GLIMPSES OF GOD

...IN YOU AND ME

KATHLEEN OSBELT

CONTENTS

This book is dedicated to the administrators, volunteers and staff of Francis House whose love has made a difference for thousands of people living their last days in our care.

To the many families who have placed their loved ones in the care of the Francis House Family.

Finally, to those who have died at Francis House and are watching over us. Now you know you always were "a glimpse of God."

ACKNOWLEDGMENTS

I thank my sisters, Joan, Pat, Janet and Joette who have been a source of encouragement throughout my ministry at Francis House and have been active volunteers at our home for those who are dying.

To those who assisted in the founding of Francis House particularly Sister Eloise Emm, Msgr. J. Robert Yeazel and Yvonne.

To my sisters in the Sisters of St. Francis of the Neumann Communities, and friends who have supported my ministry to care for those who are sick and dying.

INTRODUCTION

Several years ago I was on my way to give a talk that would begin a Lenten Retreat. The reflection was on the opening Gospel of the season, Luke 4: 1–13, the Temptation in the Desert. My reflections had been well pored over the week before as I contemplated the whole scene: Jesus, going out into that wilderness, besieged by one demon after another. My meditations on this Scripture text examined each temptation individually. They were the old favorites—wealth, power, and prestige. In the talk I had prepared there were some examples which I hoped would show that there are contemporary applications for the Lenten journey for today's Christian.

The church was a half-hour drive from my home and I remember it being a sunny morning, so I relished the time to enjoy God's beauty along the way. The distance also allowed me time to go over the talk in my head. Usually when I address a group I put a few words of the outline on a tiny 2" x 2" sheet of paper to make sure I do not go off on a tangent, which can easily happen. I had plenty of extra time, having left the house early, and I was calm because my talk was well prepared. Just as I was about to review the temptations of Jesus in the desert, this wave of insight washed over me from someplace outside of me, or from deep within me. I felt an urgency to go back and look over the earlier chapter of Luke, to open and read Luke 3. "Why? I am already prepared," I thought. "This is crazy."

The message continued: "Stop and read Luke, chapter 3!" The voice was too strong for me to ignore. Now I was chiding myself for having left the house so early. See! You've got too much time! Now you're imagining things! With reluctance I pulled the car over to the side of the road and reached for my Bible. I opened to Luke 3:31. Jesus had just been baptized and was at prayer when the sky opened and a voice was heard: "You are my beloved Son, on you my favor rests." The beginning of Luke 4:3 quotes the devil as saying to Jesus: "IF you are the Son of God" then the food, material possessions, and power will follow if the devil is worshipped. Why didn't I see that before, that great big "IF"? The connection was made.

All the temptations Jesus had in the desert were based on denying who Jesus is, the Son of God, the Beloved! As if that wasn't enough, the devil had to tempt him with food, material goods, and power. Isn't that the underlying reason why we surround ourselves with all kinds of supposed needs? Perhaps we are tempted not to believe this good news about Jesus and about ourselves? Isn't this the deeper, foundational truth that is tested over and over again? How could we, each of us, be the beloved of God? How could you be a son or daughter of God? That is just reserved for Jesus. Not true! Our very existence gives proof of our "belovedness." You exist; therefore, you are the beloved of God.

This experience on the road that day led to a theme which has found itself woven in all my musings, readings, lectures, and searches for truth. It has been key to my own understanding of who we are and how we are to move in this world. The Good News is even better than we could ever imagine! You are "the beloved!" You reflect God's infinite faces of goodness when you act out of your true loving nature. The stories in this volume give us glimpses of how that wonderful mystery of God dwelling in us pops out into clear sight, most just happen to take place in a home where people are dying

—Francis House. It is a place where the truth of God's existence can be a little louder than in other places. Francis House is a home and extended family for those who are terminally ill. It is a loving environment in which people can live their last days in dignity surrounded by the unconditional love of God. In that eleventh-hour light, truth sits on the bed of each dying person, available for all of us to take notice.

The reflections in this book are offered to open your mind, whet your spiritual appetite, and give you a desire for the "more," the more of who you really are beneath the crust of your being, and the goodness that lies within. One thing is for sure, the most important part of this book comes after you read each chapter, the part not written. It is what happens in the time and space you give to just sitting with God. If you're a risk taker, and if you desire God, be faithful and allow time for God to break into your story. Be generous enough to give yourself a routine of daily quiet time spent just sitting with the Spirit of God—your Spirit!

Since that day along the side of the road with the Gospel of Luke, I have had the privilege of hosting many retreats and giving many presentations. The greatest blessing has been my ministry over thirty years of sitting at the bedside of those who are dying at Francis House. Throughout my years of ministry, I have been convinced that most people do not realize what it means to be made in the image and likeness of God. They do not think that God is madly in love with them. They do not feel worthy of love. In essence, most of us do not know who we are. The musings within the following chapters are attempts to encourage us all to embrace our real identity as made in the image and likeness of God.

YOU ARE THE BELOVED

It was not you who chose me, it was I who chose you to go forth and bear fruit.

—John 15:16

This is my Beloved Son on whom my favor rests.

—Matthew 17:5

I had an obsession with getting good grades that started in grammar school. My goal was not only to get good grades, but to get the best grades. Perhaps this drive came from a desire to please my mother whose question was always: "How does your mark compare with others?" I studied diligently and memorized whatever my brain cells could hold. My frenzy for perfect grades continued through high school, and was especially strong in my junior and senior years. During those years I held a part-time job as a department store clerk. On Mondays, Thursdays, and Fridays I would arrive home at 9:30 p.m. then start my homework. Burning the midnight oil was rewarded by straight A's, but at what cost? How sad that I thought it was all so important to be at the top, to put myself under all that stress. Really, who asks you, years after graduation, if you got an A in every class? But you see, I thought I had to prove myself, my worth, my reason for being. I had to please my mother and my teachers, and achieve my goal! In those days I never would have believed I was the "Beloved of God." It seemed truer that perhaps I would be worthy of love if I got the best grades.

In my adult years I still strove to be the best, although the goal changed: first to be the best teacher, then the best chaplain, in short, the best at whatever! Then, maybe then, I would be worthy enough to be one of God's beloved daughters. What fueled all that anxiety? I heard many times growing up that I was a "surprise" to my parents, born in their later years. How did I react to that? Well if I was not planned and was a surprise, then I had better make people think the surprise was good. They certainly loved me and cared for me, but there was this little, persistent voice in my head that said I had to earn their love since I was not a part of their family plan. If I had to earn my parents' love, I most certainly had to earn God's love. I was blind to the fact that it was already accomplished. You and I are the Beloved no matter what we do or don't do..

Long before your appearance on this earth you were planned by God. "... for God chose us in Christ before the foundation of the world....(Ephesians 1:4) We existed in the mind of God before creation! There is no one who delighted more in your birth than God! You didn't have to do a thing, just show up. Have you seen the look on new parents' faces when a long-awaited baby is finally born? Sheer joy! Pure delight! The parents are elated because this child came forth from them. They see themselves when they look into the face of their child. That is how God feels about you. When God looks at you God sees a reflection of all that is good and hopeful and right.

Jonah, a teen with very little self-esteem, often

wondered if life had any meaning. He was fearful, afraid of venturing forth and doing anything new. He admitted to having many dark days. None of this was surprising because he had no one to tell him he was loved when he was small. Quite the opposite, in fact, as Jonah was abused as a child and struggled to see any value or worth in his life. I met Jonah in a hospital psychiatric ward shortly after he had tried to take his life. He was thirteen. Over the course of three months the psychiatrists were able to release Jonah into the capable hands of a counselor who continued the course of healing for Jonah. Eventually, Jonah learned that he was good and worthy of a life full of potential.

There are many ways in which God intercedes and gives another chance for those who miss the message that they are the Beloved. God always finds ways to tell someone that they are very much loved, for "not a single sparrow falls to the ground without God noticing" (Matthew 10:29). How much more valuable is each one of us having been made in the image of God!

Another person I think of who was most in need of knowing how loved she was is Carrie. For many of Carrie's teen years, her mother was sick with cancer. Eventually, her mom was admitted to Francis House for the last three months of her life. During that time,

Carrie had only her boyfriend to share her grief with. Shortly before her mom died, Carrie felt she had to tell her that she was pregnant. Of course, mom was not pleased, but despite this, she consoled Carrie, affirming that she trusted Carrie to make the right decisions. Carrie's mom died, and soon after, Carrie's boyfriend lost interest. Carrie was alone and pregnant, full of fears and questions about what to do. But with the help of the folks at Francis House and a friend of her mom's, Carrie saw her way to carry the baby full term and then gave the baby to adoptive parents. But the losses—her mother, her boyfriend, her baby—all weighed heavily on her. The burden led Carrie to want to end it all. She made several attempts on her life. But after two years, Carrie found a healthy way to mourn her losses and begin to investigate the beautiful person she is. Today, Carrie is on her way to recognizing herself as "the beloved." She has gone to college and has a very good job.

There are many of us, young and old, who need a reminder that we are God's wonderful creation, packed with every good thing God wanted us to have that we might reveal a piece of God on this earth. We need to know we are stuffed with goodness. We have all had some hard times in our lives, times when we felt abandoned, isolated, down on our luck. So many people feel the pain of rejection, disappointment, and failure—even despite a determination to succeed. But God would say to each of us, "You are my beloved, trust my love." None of us is ever alone in any of those discouraging moments. We are accompanied through every dark passage, even though we do not know it. God is pleased with each of us for not giving up. God loves us with a greater love than we can imagine.

DURING JOHN'S baptism of Jesus, the skies opened up and a voice was heard: "This is my Beloved Son, in whom I am well pleased" (Luke 3:22). When I pondered these words, it struck me that there is a direct link between these words, heard that day, and the words of the devil tempting Jesus in the desert: "IF you are the Son of God, command this stone to become bread" (Luke 4:3). Jesus was drawn to the desert to examine what it meant to be the Beloved of God. He had to struggle with this great affirmation and how it stood against the priorities and temptations of this world. When Jesus came to be baptized, he hadn't done anything yet! It took thirty years for Jesus to come into the public for ministry, and even then we see Him still growing into who He was. Likewise, we are always growing into who we truly are. Thomas Merton, a Catholic monk, theologian, and mystic would say we are growing into our "true selves." It takes many reminders before we believe in our true selves, in our "beloved-ness." It's like sitting along the seashore while it is engulfed in a thick fog. We cannot see anything, but once in a while the sun breaks through and clarifies what is around us. There will be events and happenings, people we encounter, things we hear or read that slowly shed light on our darkness that we may come to realize that we, too, are the beloved of God.

LET'S return to the Jordan for a moment. When John the Baptist was asked by the people who he was, his response was quite counter-cultural in that he did not give the name of his father as was expected. His father's name would indicate his blood line, clan, and home-town. People would then know where he came from. But John gives reference to neither lineage nor geography. His identity is fixed to the person of Jesus. "I am a voice crying out in the wilderness; make straight the way of the Lord" (Luke 3:4). John sees himself in the light of Jesus, not separate from Jesus. The next time we are at a gathering where introductions are made, we could answer with, "Oh, I'm one loved by God," or "I am one of Jesus's friends." That probably won't happen, understandably. But more importantly, do we act as one loved by God? Is there openness to God, is there a trust? Is there mutuality? We could each remind ourselves: God loves me, I love God; God is giving to me, I am giving to God; God is listening to me, I am listening to God. This is what it means to be in a covenant with God, a relationship that is reciprocal and mutually giving.

The last of the five classes for new Francis House volunteers is a role-playing session. One of the proposed situations is with a resident who seems to be very religious. She says a rosary, gets a weekly visit from her parish priest, and has a prayer book on her night stand. In the middle of a conversation with a volunteer she asks: "Why do you think God is punishing me?" Invariably, the new volunteers will want to immediately defend God. I then teach about the universal question when we are faced with suffering: Why? "Why did this happen to me?" Or "Why did my child get into drugs?" or "Why did my job get cut?" It's the natural response to what we can't explain. It indicates powerlessness and highlights our limitations. The key point I try to make in class is that it is more important that we do what God would do, which is to simply validate that person's feelings, thereby modeling and reflecting God's unconditional love. This is how we listen to the Francis House residents and love them where they are. This is what God is asking of us. God is saying: "I made you in my image. Will you be that image for others?" The first step is to understand that God planned you. Even if you were a surprise to your parents, God planned your coming. God brought you forth that you might be God's image for others to see and know how very great God's love is.

JESUS, THE FIRST AMONG THE "BELOVEDS," was planned for all time, and through Jesus we are shown the way back home to God. It was never sin that occasioned Jesus's coming, it was to bring forth all things in love and draw it all back to God in that love. From the dawn of time, it was love that ignited the action of God. The desire of that love is you, is me! God desired that you and I would grow in the experience of love, and so God provides for you a way. It is never your sin that God sees, but your potential, your goodness, your beauty. God loves you in your littleness. "God looked at everything he had made, and he found it very good." (Genesis 1:31) As you grow in awareness of this truth, the image of God grows in you and is reflected back to the world.

A Meditation

THINK of a time when you felt truly loved and understood. Remember a time when you were shown love and acceptance. What was going on in your life at the time? Where were you? Who was there? That experience was just a whisper of the love that God has for you.

2

YOU ARE GOD'S DREAM

Hosanna! Blessed is he who comes in the name of the Lord.

—John 12:13

Do you know who you are? You are God's dream. I'll just bet you never thought that! Do you know that God has dreamed of you for all time? God dreamed of a you then made you in God's image. You have probably heard that since you were a little kid and probably often wondered how everyone could be made in God's image when they looked and acted so differently. I know. I wondered that, too. But having a best friend with twelve brothers and sisters helped me to understand this a bit. My siblings numbered only three so I was always amazed when I went to her house. All those kids in my friend's family came from just two parents, and all of them had very distinct personalities. But yes, they all had the same family traits and some of the same mannerisms. Their parents' images could be seen in each and every one, one a little stronger in that trait, the other a little stronger in a different one. But God's image, now that's another thing! We don't think too frequently about that.

For just a moment, ponder the fact that you came through the love of God, tumbling into this particular century, into the town where your life started, to the parents who raised you. God arranged all this for you! Now perhaps you are saying: "Thanks very much, but why couldn't I have been born to someone else or in another time?" No, this unique situation which is yours is no accident. God's fingerprint is all over you and everything about you; your gifts, the people who bless your life, the opportunities you get, it's all quite deliberate. God is all love, and love is ever-giving. You too were a part of God's gracious giving. G. K. Chesterton once said it was as if God was making a field of daisies, and they were so delightful that God kept saying "More, more."[1] Isn't that what you hear from a child when you bounce the little one on your foot? In between the giggles, that child says with delight, "More, more." But it wasn't just for "more, more" that you came—it was to have a YOU in the world. A once-in-a-lifetime, never-to-be-repeated YOU. God wanted to express God's self as YOU.

In attending a talk given by activist, Edwina Gateley, I was amused by an image she gave in saying that we are all "God drops." The breezes roll over the ocean, she explained, and pick up moisture creating tiny drops of water in the air. These are not the ocean, but they are small hints of the ocean. We are not God. We are "God drops." So God continues to dream of you because you came into this story of the universe and play a key role in bringing this universe, or at least the universe that you touch, to its potential. You were made in the image of the love, the goodness, the compassion, and the creativeness of God, so that you might give it away as you journey through life.

Other people may also have had dreams for you. Some of those may have been planted by God too—dreams for you to grow up well and healthy, to discover and use all of your talents, to be happy, good, successful. Perhaps some of those dreams came from dreams they had for their own lives and never got to complete. My own mother wanted to go to college but never did because her parents did not have the funds to send her.

Higher education was a luxury in her day. So throughout my own schooling, I was challenged to get the highest grades possible so I could be eligible for a scholarship. My father who never went beyond grammar school, did not have the same dream for me. He simply hoped I would get a good job so that I wouldn't have to struggle all my life to make ends meet as he had. But both shared one dream for me and expressed it at varying times—that I be happy. Isn't that every loving parent's dream? It certainly is our first Parent's dream for us—God's dream.

There are others who have dreams for you along the way. Among them may have been a teacher who influenced you, a coach, an aunt or uncle, a church leader, or the director of a club or organization. Perhaps someone you worked for had a dream for you to excel in your job. Whoever they have been and in whatever moment they entered your life, they were participants in activating God's "Great Dream" for you.

God has planted "dream seeds" in you as well! You must allow them to open and blossom as you pursue a career, accomplish a task, acquire a long-awaited possession, achieve a degree of training or education, make a vow, have children. Dreams can be as immediate as a trip to another city or as distant and tedious as reaching a life goal. God's dream continues as your life unfolds.

Our dreams directly affect the lives of others. You may have dreams for your friends, wanting them to live up to their potential. You may have dreams for your children, for your family, for your church group, your company, or some organization you've joined. Some dreams may propel you to act, some may fall on dry ground and simply wither.

While I was a hospital chaplain, I had daily contact with those who were acutely and terminally ill. It was during that time that the seeds of a dream were planted in me. In the late 1980's, a large percent of people died in the hospital because there were very few homecare agencies and no palliative care units or hospice homes. Still today in many of our cities, over half of all deaths occur in the hospital. While I was witnessing all those deaths, I began to hear a voice in me asking: "Why isn't there a better place for people to die? A place that is more homelike, with quilts, soft chairs with colorful cushions, framed photographs and favorite trinkets, with the sounds of neighbors and children, of singing and laughing, all creating an environment more conducive to comfort. Why does a dying person who is receiving no curative treatment have to have vital signs taken every four hours and their food served on trays instead of on dishes? Why must their precious little time be jarred with the blast of "Code Blue" over the hospital intercom? Why is it that a patient's only other option is a nursing home if they have no one to take them home? Why is there no one to hear their "Why me?"

I began to dream of a home where individuals who are dying could spend their last days in peace, surrounded by activity and life.

At that time, these were just seeds planted in my heart. I did not act. I got no further than wishing for such a home. Years later I was asked to work in an office, taking on administrative responsibilities. In no time at all, I found myself missing the pastoral practice I once had. I longed for the relationships with people who were sick and needed companionship. I yearned to work with others in the care-giving professions.

One evening in 1987 at a festival, sitting on a curb and sipping a cold drink with a friend, I shared my desire to take on some pastoral volunteering. She suggested I look into working with the AIDS Task Force because they were in great need of help. She further explained that there was a six-week training course for those who wanted to be a "buddy" to someone with AIDS, an assignment I might like because it meant checking in on the person to see what their needs might be and responding to those needs as a resource, an advocate, or simply someone with a caring presence. In short she thought I might like it because I would be connecting with them as a caring human being. Now I don't normally act on such suggestions. I have to be really uncomfortable before I move. (I don't even move furniture around unless a rug is being changed!) But at this point I was feeling so much like a fish out of water that I took her advice to seek a place where I could use my skills as a pastoral minister.

I did contact the AIDS Task Force. The six-week course led me to journey first with Bill, a young man who had full-blown AIDS, a beautiful man who was both gentle and loving. His once powerful physique had wasted away to a mere ninety pounds, but there was an inner strength that kept him cheerful to his very last breath in the emergency room. My companionship with Bill lasted only four months before he went on to God, but it was enough to not only teach me about the prejudice a gay male experiences, not to mention one who has AIDS, but it also taught me about my own discomfort with his lifestyle and the disease, and helped me to grapple with those issues.

Two months passed and I was assigned to companion a young woman whose name was Yvonne. Yvonne was forty-two, had a job and a small apartment, and the friendship of two gay men. These two men came into Yvonne's life when all three of them were in a rehabilitation center in the Adirondack Mountains.

Each had an addiction, the two men, Bob and Jerry, to alcohol, and Yvonne to was addicted to heroin. Yvonne was exposed to drugs while growing up in Harlem in an extremely abusive household with an addicted mother who used to beat her children with extension cords. Yvonne hooked up with the first guy who was nice to her, but even this relationship spiraled with drugs and abuse. Yvonne became desperately addicted, the courts took her children from her, and she found herself forced into that rehabilitation center in the Adirondacks by order of a compassionate judge.

Once rehabilitated, Yvonne and her two new friends, Bob and Bill, were released from the center at the same time. Bob and Bill invited her to start over again Syracuse where she could get a job and live far from her past. For the first time, Yvonne was a liberated woman! Little did she know that a deadly virus was following her from her long-forgotten days of shared needles. By the time I met Yvonne she was diagnosed but still independently living and working. However, in a matter of weeks, she had an acute event of amnesia because the disease had affected her brain. While riding a bus to work one day, she suddenly had no idea where she was going or even who she was. She became hysterical. The bus driver pulled over, dialed 911 and Yvonne was taken away in an ambulance. She was admitted into a local hospital and was given drug therapy to stabilize her and lessen the effects of the virus. Within a week, Yvonne was strong enough to go to a nursing home, and would have been released, but at that time not one nursing home had room. For eight months not one nursing home "had room"! I called and called. I was on that phone every day but this was 1988, and everyone was panicked just by the word 'AIDS.' Yvonne spent her birthday, Christmas, Easter, and Thanksgiving in that isolation room in the hospital. All that changed in her room were the decorations that Bill, Bob, and I put up. Today, in the United States, with the new protocols available, AIDS tends to be a long-term disease. But thirty years ago, it was a fearful contagion and death sentence. I was angry that a human being in our country was so shunned. That righteous anger that I experienced led me finally to action. I opened, with the assistance of many people, a home for persons who are dying. Little did I know it then, but this was the path God had been taking me through to be a vehicle for God's dream of justice.

You see, you are a bit of God here on earth. You are what God dreamed of for all time and who God continues to dream through. Everyone has dreams of who they would like to be, of what they would like to do, and of what they would like to have. In you is God's dream that only you can fulfill.

Some dreams are as big as a lifetime. It was that way for Gandhi. Mahatma Gandhi kept sifting through his life experiences, comparing them to what he read in the Koran, the Bible, and the Bhagavad Gita. To him, these words of wisdom all pointed to expressing a deep love for humanity. Gandhi set out on a dream of loving every single person, including his enemies and those who hurt him or hurt those around him. He began to experiment with how far he could push the edges of his love.[2] The God dream of love began to take shape in his life. This is the way it happens; this is how God's dream takes hold.

You may have seen a Dream Catcher somewhere perhaps hung in a window, on a wall over a bed, or from a car's rear-view mirror (although I don't see how that helps one's vision!). Some I have seen in office cubicles. They're pretty—a circle that has a net inside it and is adorned with beads and feathers. But there is a legend behind them.

The legend of the Dream Catcher originated with a Lakota spiritual leader who had a high mountain vision. In his vision, the great teacher of wisdom, Iktomi, appeared in the form of a spider. Iktomi spoke in the sacred language and, picking up the elder's hoop feathers, horsehair, and bead offerings, he began to spin a web. Iktomi spoke to the elder about the cycles of life.

We begin as infants, move into childhood, adulthood, and then old age, where we must be taken care of as infants again, completing the cycle. In each life segment, there are good and evil forces. If you listen to good forces, they will steer you on the right path. If you listen to bad forces, you will be steered in the wrong direction and may be hurt. These forces, Iktomi explained, can help you or interfere with the harmony of nature. Iktomi then wove a web through the hoop. When he finished, he gave the webbed hoop to the elder, saying, "The web is a perfect circle with a hole in the center. Use the web to help your people reach their goals, making good use of their ideas, dreams, and visions. If you believe in the Great Spirit, the web will catch your good ideas and the bad ones will go through the hole." The elder passed on the vision. The people used the Dream Catcher to sift their dreams and visions. The good ones were captured in the web of life and carried with the people. The evil dreams and visions dropped through the hole in the center and were no longer a part of their lives.[3]

Just as the Lakota were given this dream catcher, every person born has been given the Spirit of God. This Spirit assists us with the inspiration needed to use the gifts that are ours. The Spirit of God breathes thoughts and ideas, stirs emotions and heightens senses, that we may become more attuned to God's dream, and siphon off those which are self-centered dreams. That Spirit works through our conscience, giving us energy for the good and warning us as to what is evil. When we pursue a dream which will result in good, it is a small revelation of the good God. It is another way in which the "Good News" continues. The grace given us to bring that dream into reality is part of the dynamic unfolding of the Original Intent. By Original Intent, I mean the purpose for which you, and I, and all creation were made. God, the Origin of all, intends that all things become united with God in God's love. The foundation of all life is this greater love which keeps us in existence and which brings us closer to the Original Intent, the Great Dream. God's love for all creation and God's dream of the experience of love for all of us has been poured into you. You were created out of this incredible overwhelming love, planned for all time, to be born at an assigned time to a particular set of parents, situated in the reality of a special moment and place. You were brought forth in this Divine love, and given a life that is meant to be lived in that love and reflect that love. You were sent to live fully with the gifts you have been given as part of the great plan, that Original Intent, which is to bring all things into one in God. The gifts you have will draw you and those you influence towards God's dream.

There have been many things that you have wanted to do with your life. But when you take the time to truly listen to your heart, you will be, step by step, on the way to the dreams that are bigger than you. It's your destiny and your way to fulfillment.

A Meditation

THINK about the dreams you have had growing up. Have you noticed their effects on your life since having them? What about the dreams others have had for you? What has happened to them? Spend a few moments thanking God for working any dreams for good into your life.

3

YOU ARE THE LIGHT OF GOD

Your light must shine before others so that they may see goodness in your acts and give praise to your heavenly father.

—Matthew 5:16

he light refracted by a prism splashes across the surface with all the primary colors. Each of us is a prism for God's light, and in the particular way God's light shines through us reveals the uniqueness of each person. There is a wonder-filled array of God's gifts that shine through every created being. Each of us was born of light, meaning we are spiritual beings, given a body through which our spirit can be expressed. To follow Jesus is to follow his light and his spirit. His light is shown in the ways that he relates to the world around him, how he shows mercy, how He reaches out to the outcast, and how he calls others back to life through love. We are made of the same light. When our actions are motivated by love, it is our light being revealed in its own unique way. We come from the Light and we go back to the Light.

Just before opening Francis House, I attended a lecture presented by Raymond A. Moody, psychiatrist and the author of *Life after Life*.[1]

He spoke about his findings after interviewing thousands of people around the globe who had life after death experiences. Many of those interviewed said that they had an experience of being taken out of their bodies and drawn into a kind of tunnel through which they were moving toward a bright light. Usually there was someone in the light waiting to greet them: Jesus, a parent, a spouse, a child, someone who they recognized and loved.

HAVING HAD thirty years at Francis House, I have been privileged to sit at the bedside of many as they took their last breath. Ethel had been at Francis House for a month. She was a quiet woman, gracious and patient with her disease process. She enjoyed sitting in the living room just outside her bedroom because it had lovely windows while her bedroom had none. On Ethel's last day of life, as I sat by her bedside, she asked me in a whisper, "Please pull the shade because the light is too bright." There was no shade because there was no window in the room. She was seeing a light far beyond us. I told her it was time for her to leave us. Ethel peacefully closed her eyes and gave in to the call to enter that light.

More of our Francis House residents than I can record have spoken of seeing angels in the room, or family members who were deceased, or who asked "Who is that?" while pointing to a place above us. Recently an eight-month-old was in the bedroom of her actively dying great grandmother, Lucille. Lucille's daughter opened the window in the bedroom "so that the angels can come take mom." The baby began waving at someone with a smile. No one visible was standing where the baby was directing her wave, between the window and Lucille. A few moments later, Lucille died. I told the baby's mother that babies have fewer filters than we adults have, and can see what we do not see.

Animals, too, sense spiritual beings around us. We had a cat at Francis House, Bootsy, who would go into the bedroom of the person who was going to die next.

She just sat near the bed. She was always correct, but made people very uncomfortable. Needless to say, we did not keep Bootsy very long. She unnerved the staff.

There is a prayer practice of holding another person in the Light. The prayer begins by acknowledging that we are all connected, brothers and sisters in this one universe. Our very being affects every other being for good or for ill. We believe from scientific research that the source of this connection is energy. Energy creates energy. We are capable of both positive and negative energy. You may have heard it said that some people suck the air out of a room, or conversely, that a whole room lights up when a particular person walks into it. One reflects negative energy, and the other reflects positive energy. The thoughtful and faith-filled prayer of Jesus was positive, creative energy. It transformed and transcended time and space. Our prayers can do the same. Positive, loving thoughts and energy can create what is positive, good, and peace-filled. We go to prayer believing that God's love and light are already within us and within all creation. In our prayer, we spend time imagining ourselves surrounded by the beautiful light of God's presence. Then we allow ourselves to see images of others who are in need of love, healing, and compassion. We take the pain of the person, group, nation, creation, whatever we are praying for into us and hold it in God's light and love. We ask that pain to be transformed, trusting that God's healing, transforming light will work through us.

I was seven years old when my father took me to see the movie, *Frankenstein*. Had he read Dr. Spock's books on how to raise children, he might have learned that this was not helpful to my development, but this, in my father's estimation, was an enjoyable afternoon. To this day I remember my terror as I lay in bed that night, obsessively praying the "Hail Mary" so that Frankenstein would not come out from under my bed. Once the light was turned on in the living room next to my bedroom I was relieved and could see that Frankenstein was not under my bed. Once there was light, I could finally fall asleep. The light brought peace to my agitated spirit and security to my trembling heart. The light was a comfort.

Christ comes as light to the world. In the Gospel of John is the proclamation: "Whatever came to be in him, found life, life for the light of all, (inclusive language adapted)men. The light shines on in darkness, a darkness that did not overcome it." (John 1:4). Christ is the light of God within each of us. Just as light reveals the magnificence of a stained-glass window, so too does the light within a person tell of the brilliance of that person's soul.

Kaleidoscopes have always captured my attention. When held to the light they present a multitude of colors and shapes dissolving and blossoming into one another. Without the light they show only opaque and hardly discernible images. We are like kaleidoscopes. Christ's light shining through our goodness and love makes for a brilliance in this world where darkness would attempt to overcome our light. When we sit in silence, contemplating and soaking in the presence of God, we might begin to recognize the beauty of God around us, the touch of God in all things created. God's light and goodness shine through all that has come from the hand of God. For the person who does not stand back to see and to admire the world simply becomes a place created for our use and unfortunately, sometimes for abuse.

In an inspired reflection on contemplation, Henry Nouwen, in his book *Clowning in Rome*, Nouwen sites an observation from Thomas Merton that the contemplative person as one who moves from sees opaqueness to seeing transparency, seeing the transparency of God in all things.[2] The one who does not live a reflective life sees the created world as opaque, sees time as opaque, and who sees life as a burden, "I have no time." There is never enough time for this person. It only means deadlines and rushing and frenzy. The contemplative one views time as transparent, meaning that in all events and moments there are opportunities to see God at work in the world. The contemplative one sees nature in the same way. Every aspect of the world around us is transparent in that we can see through each to the Creator. The one who sees opaquely uses and abuses nature for his or her own gain. Missing are the respect and awe deserving of something that speaks of God.

The same goes for how we see one another. A person has all the beauty and wonder of body, mind, and spirit because he or she is made in the image of God and is a most transparent temple, the holding place of God. Those who do not see the light can never penetrate the holiness of another person. Just take a look at our newspapers and magazines who exploit people as an opportunity for gossip, scandal, and sensationalism. We can look at ourselves and how we speak about one another with labels like "that poor thing," "she is a loser," "they're all terrorists." Our conversations are full of labels and sweeping generalizations. Disregarding and demeaning an individual ignores the light within them, betrays the light within us, and closes the promise of goodness and beauty.

When we see with contemplation, we reflect and generate the light of God. To behold life is to lift it in our hands and look upon it as sacred. To look upon the sacred is to bring light into the eye, the light which comes from the soul. When we allow the light to be extinguished, not only does the darkness surround us, the darkness buries itself deep within us as well.

A Meditation

WHEN YOU GET up in the morning, look to the sun of the new day breaking on the horizon. It does not happen because you will it so. And you don't make it set in the evening. If you ignore the sun, you will miss the natural light streaming across the earth. But when you give it your full attention, you welcome the sun's light into you and you become completely absorbed into the light. Meditate on this. Bring to the light your full attention, for this is the way of God's light. You become a beacon of God's light by becoming aware of God's presence within and about you. Breathe in that light, and breathe it out to the world. Carry that Light around with you all day.

4

YOU ARE GOD'S HEALING

As you go, make this announcement: "The reign of God is at hand!" Cure the sick, raise the dead, heal the leprous, and expel demons. The gift you have received, give as a gift.

—Matthew 10:7

*I*n Quebec, Canada, there is a shrine dedicated to St. Anne de Beaupré. My mother and father planned a family visit there when I was six years old. I loved the ride, the beautiful grounds of the shrine, and the gigantic statues. But I was terribly disturbed when I saw all the crutches fastened to the pillars inside the shrine church. My young mind was full of questions: Whose crutches were those? Why did they leave them there? My mother explained that the people who used those crutches and braces left them because they no longer needed them. They had been healed by prayer. I was filled with even more questions. How did that happen? What did they do to get healed? What prayers do you have to say?

Years later when our family was vacationing in Canada again, we made a visit to St. Joseph's Oratory in Montreal. (What can I say? My mother was into Catholic vacations.) Once again I was amazed at what I saw. There were crutches, braces and canes of every sort attached to pillars everywhere. I read the testimonies of those who had been cured and thought about how incredibly happy those people must have been.

In 1993, I made my own pilgrimage to St. Joseph's when I was visiting with a friend a few hours away. This, visit, however, was for my own healing. I was crippled with fear at the time. Francis House was in jeopardy because it had been reported to the state that we were operating what was the equivalent of a nursing home without a license. At that time there were no free-standing hospice homes in New York State, and it was quite possible the State Health Department would close Francis House. We had worked so hard to establish it, and now it was threatened. It had been two months since the state inspectors had been to Francis House and with each passing day that I had no response from them, I grew more worried. There were sleepless nights, much distraction, and lots of anxious eating—my coping mechanism when I'm tired or worried. The pilgrimage to St. Joseph's shrine was to ask God for a healing of my anxiety. This burden of worry had to be given over and replaced with trust. That is what I prayed would happen. I did not stop worrying the moment I stood up from the kneeler but I was far more confidant when my companion said, "It's going to be OK. Francis House is a good thing and God will protect it." A week later, my mind actually grasped the words of one of the Board Members who also chided me to trust. He said, "God will not abandon this project," and I believed it. There was no longer that terrible nagging worry. One month later we had a visit from the local representative of the State Health Department who actually commended our work and said he wished there were more places like Francis House!

This is frequently how healing happens. God, who truly does love us more than we can imagine, enfolds us, softens us, give us the grace to believe that all will be well. Julian of Norwich, an English mystic, is noted for saying precisely that: "All shall be well. All manner of things shall be well." She came to this through a vision:

"He showed me something small, no bigger than a hazelnut, lying in the palm of my hand, as it seemed to me, and it was as round as a ball. I looked at it with the eye of my understanding and thought: What can this be? I was amazed that it could last, for I thought that because of its littleness it would suddenly have fallen into nothing. And I was answered in my understanding: It lasts and always will, because God loves it; and thus everything has being through the love of God."[1]

You are called to be that source of healing for others just as my friend and that Board Member were for me. In the words of the old spiritual, "He's got the whole world in His hands." Indeed, God has the whole world because all is in God. Every one of us needs to know that God holds us through every tough moment. God has our back, so to speak. Each of us will find ourselves listening at some time to a person who is in pain and needing to know God is there. God needs us to be a healing agent by conveying our confidence in a loving God who cares deeply. There will be people who need to know that God wants to heal them. When people do confidently pray for healing there is sometimes the expectation that God will heal them in a particular manner. But God knows what is most needed, and that is what God attends to, although it may not be exactly the healing they envisioned for themselves.

When the paralyzed man was lowered through the roof of the home where Jesus was speaking, the first thing Jesus said to him was, "Your sins are forgiven you." (Luke 7:48) We understand sin as separation from God, therefore, it makes sense that this was the greatest healing. The paralyzed man saw Jesus, Jesus saw him, and they connected. There was no more separation. When we are separated from God, we are separated from ourselves as well, and that is the greatest sickness. I once heard a speaker say that a woman had not been to confession in many years, and there had been so much to say that she did not know how to begin. The confessor said simply, "Just say you have not been yourself."

People are often a bit startled when I say that I have seen many healthy people die at Francis House. Then I explain that it does not mean that these residents' bodies were not ill. It refers to their spiritual health. These are the residents who are at peace and who know themselves in God. Helen was riddled with cancer, had been through both radiation and chemotherapy over the course of several years, and yet she had a smile for everyone who entered her room. She spent her days busily making ornaments specific to every person on the staff. Helen was physically very sick but her spirit was radiant.

Tom, dying of an aggressive brain tumor, came out to the dining room table every morning so he could play poker with Blake, a young volunteer, so he could tease and challenge Blake, and offer him some life's wisdom.

There are others who feel separated from family, from humanity, and from God. I urge our volunteers to give a quality presence to our residents because their presence may be what breaks through that isolation caused by so many losses. The volunteers are often the ones who melt the fear that accompanies the imminence of death. Some residents who I have sat with have worked through guilt and shame related to broken relationships, including their relationship with God. Being present and listening with love and compassion facilitates the return of some dignity to these residents. Healing comes with loving, and God is always there in the loving.

We all have areas in our own life that need healing. God asks us to move into a certainty that God is right there in the middle of our "mess" and has no intentions of moving out. When we truly choose to believe this, we will be a source of healing for others. Part of the Clinical Pastoral Education training which prepares a person to be a chaplain to those who are sick requires the trainee to examine and share the pieces of his or her own life that are broken and feel dark. It is only in going into our own shadows that we are ready to walk with another into theirs and facilitate God's healing. The best healers are those who know God's hand upon their lives bringing them through every valley and stormy night.

There are thirty-five accounts of Jesus healing someone in the New Testament and references to whole crowds that were healed. It is unfortunate that we do not see the physical healings as minor events in a beautiful movement of spiritual healing. What about the hundreds who were healed when Jesus proclaimed, "Blessed are you poor, for the Kingdom shall be yours. Blessed are you who weep, you shall laugh"? (Luke 6: 20,21) He blessed the persecuted, the oppressed, those who were rejected and shunned, and he made them whole. With the invitation: "Come to me all you who are weary and find life burdensome, and I shall give you rest," (Matthew 11:28-30) who could not hear Jesus's love and mercy and feel his compassionate heart?

We are made in the image of the Source of all healing. On our journey through life, God will confront us with people who need to know they are blessed, they are good, they are whole, and they are worthy. There will be those who need to hear "all shall be well." They all need healing and hopefully we will be there to assist in that healing. The example of our confidence in the God who holds all things together will be just what the "doctor ordered," that is to say, what God desires.

A Meditation

Picture a beautiful broken vase. It is valuable but needs to be mended. You are that vase. Tell God what broke you or is breaking you now. Ask for the healing you desire. Now, with all trust, thank God for that healing, believing God wants you to be whole. God will fill that broken part with light making the entire vase more beautiful.

5

YOU ARE GOD'S GENEROSITY

Give and it shall be given to you. Good measure pressed down, shaken together, running over, will they pour into the fold of your garment.

—Luke 6:38

There is all graciousness and generosity in God and it is poured out on us every moment. Those who are "awake" can see God's generosity flowing out over us. They can say "Bless us, O Lord, and these, Thy gifts" as they behold a beautiful landscape, a newborn, a work of art, a sunrise. Each day is jam packed with God's gifts. Not one of them has been or could be earned. All we have to do is receive them and give thanks to our Benefactor. Such awareness of our multiple blessings leads to a desire to share our gifts. The heart that is bursting with gratitude also wants to do something in thanksgiving to express that gratitude. That doing is often called charity, love, and generosity. We often meet people who we hold in awe because of their capacity to express the fact that their life is full of blessings. That awe is extended when we come upon someone who is not only a person of gratitude but gives freely because of it.

Rod, a retired master plumber, volunteered at Francis House for thirteen years. He saved our ministry thousands of dollars in plumbing repairs, and he organized our food pantry and kept track of its inventory. This wiry little man regaled us with stories of people he met out West and stories from his years in the construction business. He died at Francis House. At his eulogy I shared that this man of slight stature and great spirit used to name the days of the week by what he did that day: Sunday he took Larry, an elderly man, to Mass and brunch, Monday and Thursday he worked at Francis House, Tuesday was his day to help his two infirm neighbors, Wednesday was for visiting his older sisters and doing errands for them, Friday was a day for chores at home, and on Saturday he delivered food he purchased at the farmers' market or vegetables from his garden to those in need. He never boasted. In fact, I pried his schedule out of him one day because I had been trying to reach him on the phone (why are you never home?). At the luncheon after Rod's funeral, more stories of Rod came flowing out from every corner of the banquet room. We heard: "In the days of construction when we built ten-story apartment buildings, Rod, with his bandaged, ulcerated legs, would climb up to the top floor to make sure all the guys who worked that day were safely out of the building. This was before the elevators were installed. He would also be the one to work on the roof top when it was biting cold and windy." I could see the whole table of guys nodding in agreement to this testimony. Then from someone else: "He used to leave me vegetables in a bag hanging from my door knob," followed by several echoes of "Me, too!" A woman witnessed: "When my husband was out of work, Rod left a brand-new bike on our porch for our son Christmas morning." "Rod helped me with my tuition," his young niece said. "Rod made me laugh." "Rod wrote a beautiful poem for me on my birthday." "Rod told me he prayed for me daily to have courage and trust." It was a real celebration of Rod's love and charity. Everyone had a Rod story, but all those stories were a surprise to everyone else! Rod's humility overwhelmed us. People just sat there shaking their heads at Rod's incredible goodness. Talk about telling the world what God is like! I am quite sure Rod would have been uncomfortable at the applause given his life but would have rejoiced in the gathering and unified spirit in that room.

GOD'S POCKETS are emptied for us, and out spills love. In the Parable of the Prodigal Son, the Father waited every day for his son to return. When he saw his son on the horizon, the father ran, to him, an action that would have been scandalous for an elder in ancient Jerusalem. He hugged and kissed his errant son. He did not make the son give an account of his squandering. The father put his own ring on his son's finger and wrapped him in the finest robe. The father donned his son's worn feet with new shoes. Then he announced that a party would be thrown, a great big party! To the other son who was jealous he said: "Everything I have is yours!" (Luke 15:31) This loving, generous father is our God. Who could not fall in love with a God like that?

IT'S a bit of a mystery to me but it seems that the more a person becomes aware of his or her blessings, the more blessings that person receives. There are no coincidences of fate. I heard a woman respond to another who had been talking about her accomplished son saying, "Aren't you lucky?" The mother answered: "Luck has nothing to do with it. It is God blessing us." There is only God, and God's generous love holds all things in connection with each other.

Once, I was selected for a task and later learned that someone was opposed to my being chosen because I was, as she put it, "spoiled and favored." At first I was hurt. But when I took it to God, I realized she was right! I am spoiled and favored. At every turn, God is there helping me, getting me though the dark times, giving me hope for the light. Yes, I am spoiled and favored, and I pray that you will discover that you are, too. If you can see that truth, you will want to be generous, too. Are we always big-hearted? No. That's why we need to keep going back to the mirror to see how well our image reflects the one who sent us.

We are such a tenuous mix of security and fear. When we feel safe and believe that the tap of God's generous fountain will never be shut off, we feel free to give without cost. But when we are fearful we hold back, thinking that the resources might run dry. And we question: "What will be left for me?" That's a scarcity mentality, not an abundance mentality. The abundance mentality is the belief that there is always enough. Our

Italian neighbor had an abundance mentality. She, the "mother of the neighborhood," always invited people to eat. For her, there was always enough. It is fear that holds us in our small little world of "me" and "mine." No wonder Jesus said seventy-nine times: "Fear is useless; what is needed is trust" (Luke 8:50).

ON MY EIGHTH BIRTHDAY, I received a new blue bicycle. What I remember most about that bike now is that when I received it, a girl my age from up the street, Bernadette, a girl from a very poor family, asked to ride it. Emphatically I said: "No!" I had little interaction with Bernadette, and don't remember much about her, but I have never forgotten that incident, nor my lack of empathy and my selfishness. Since then I have given away two bicycles, looking to heal from my own stinginess.

Peter needed to heal too. Peter denied Jesus three times and without saying a word about the denial, Jesus gave Peter three opportunities to say he loved Jesus. It's called restitution, or in Jesus's words, salvation.

Generosity does not always come easily, especially when we are fearful, distrusting, or feeling unloved. Since we've aged, it's no longer about sharing our toys; it's about opening our lives and modeling the God who holds back nothing. Remember the grace given us and the encouragement to live the commandment of Jesus's words: "Freely you have received; freely give" (Matt.10:8). At the Last Supper, Jesus said, "This is my body given for you; do this in remembrance of me" (Luke 22:19). Jesus offered his life and asked us to do the same. He was breaking that life open for all of us. He was inviting us to do the same for one another with a generous heart.

A Meditation

Bask for a quiet moment in all the blessings you can recount. Start with images of your childhood, then move to the present. See the faces of those you knew who were models of God's generosity. Now, in all humility, recount the ways you have demonstrated that same generosity. Look ahead to tomorrow and make a commitment to be generous with whoever comes before you and in whatever situation you find yourself.

6

YOU ARE GOD'S BEAUTY

Your adornment should not be an external one: braiding the hair, wearing gold jewelry, or dressing in fine clothes, but rather the hidden character of the heart, expressed in the imperishable beauty of a gentle calm disposition, which is precious in the sight of God.

—1 Peter 3:3–4

St. Bonaventure, theologian and mystic, in his *Soul's Journey into God*, explains that there are six ways in which the soul moves to union with God.[1] One of those ways is to see God's work in all of creation as well as in the powers of one's being: the intellect, the will, and the memory. Another Franciscan mystic, Saint Angela of Foligno said: "The world is pregnant with God."[2] Both of these Franciscans lived in the thirteenth century. The idea they described, the "cosmic Christ," didn't come into wide use until the 1700s. It refers to the presence of Christ in all there is, in all matter and time in the Universe. Its primary principle is that all created things come through Christ and dwell in Christ.

Paul, in his letters to the early Church repeats the proclamation of faith often: "for from him and through him and for him all things are." (Romans 11:36) Your very existence, and that of everything, is because of Christ. God's Spirit is imbued everywhere through Christ. Those who are contemplative have eyes to see this reality and rejoice in the fact that we are surrounded by God. They can see a tree as uniquely made, down to the pattern of its leaves and the veins that punctuate them. We can immerse ourselves in God's presence by allowing ourselves to be intoxicated by the full moon's glow and speechless in the wake of a sunrise. There is something greater than ourselves in every particle of life. The heart of the one who does not notice is asleep. God's beauty is boundlessly present and waiting to be affirmed. Each day our home planet turns towards the sun. Perhaps Mother Earth is teaching us a lesson, teaching us to turn ourselves to the light of God that we may see God's face in all that is.

The more our eyes open to see beauty, the more there seems to be. For those who do not see, it is like standing in a gallery looking at a magnificent painting, seeing the contrasting colors and shapes, but missing the genius of the artist in the details. The contemplative moments we have in life are those spent in the full light of the Son, when we see clearly the beauty of every morsel of life.

We carry about in our person a mini-cosmos, a body of interrelated systems that complement and assist one another. Our bodies are magnificent reflections of God's beauty. The artist who lives in our community acclaims the body as God's masterpiece in its symmetry, its flexibility, its soft curves, and like every other creation, its uniqueness. While our features are similar, no one body duplicates another exactly; each is unique in all the world. The nurse practitioner at the doctor's office hails the beauty of the body in the genius of its workings: the mechanisms of the various biological systems and the organs in each system that all work to keep our bodies in balance, in its production and expenditure of energy and the healing ability we all have within us. Like that practitioner, God sees our true beauty and does not see our physical nor our emotional or psychological imperfections as disfigurements. It takes someone like a Mother Theresa of Calcutta to see God's beauty even in a face ravaged by disease.

In 1868, the leader of my own religious congregation, Mother Marianne Cope, said yes to a plea to help those who had leprosy, or Hansen's disease, on the Sandwich Islands, known now as the Hawaiian Islands. The people with leprosy had been banished to a secluded peninsula called Kalaupapa, attached to the island of Molokai, to live in the most miserable conditions. Father Damien had been working in the settlement, trying to transform lean-tos into houses, advocating for materials and food for the poor sick, while also caring for their physical and spiritual needs. Mother Marianne joined Father Damien, taking six other sisters with her to serve among these discarded, abandoned people. She and the sisters were greeted with the most wretched sight—a barren land of sand and mud, spotted with shacks from which deformed people hobbled. Their bodies oozed with sores and their limbs had lost their extremities with the advance of Hansen's disease. In spite of the filth, the stench, the poverty, and the seeming despair of the people, Mother Marianne saw the beauty of these people created in God's love. She restored a sense of beauty to the land by planting trees, shrubs, and flowers, which still grace that tongue of land today. Mother

Marianne sewed fashionable clothes for the young people, brought in fresh bandages for those in need, and gathered them to sing and dance, helping to reclaim the beautiful culture that was theirs.[3]

Mother Marianne was a true follower of St. Francis of Assisi. At the end of his life, when St. Francis was enduring the worst of his pain from multiple diseases that ravaged his body, he retreated to a poor shelter near the monastery of the nuns. From that place he composed the most exquisite of Italian poems, "The Canticle of Creation."[4] This is one of the greatest Italian poems ever written. The words praise Brother Sun for his beauty, Sister Moon and Stars for being bright and precious, and all elements and created things because they reflect the beauty of the Creator. Francis wrote his masterpiece from the store of God's beauty in his heart, for by this time he had gone blind.

Like Francis, Beethoven created beauty in the face of physical obstacles. He composed his most ingenious and final masterpiece, the Ninth Symphony. Its creation spanned over a decade yet the deaf Beethoven, sick and agonized, invited all humanity to sing for joy.[5] The beauty of the music was in his heart, not his ear.

Henry Nouwen, in his book *Clowning in Rome*, writes of a little boy who, over the course of a few weeks, passed by a sculptor working on a stone. With each passing the young boy saw a bit more of the sculptor's creation emerging from the stone. The boy asked the artist, "Hey, how did you know there was a lion in that stone?" The artist replied: "Because the lion was first in me."[6]

For each of us, the beauty we see around us is nothing compared to the beauty we each may have within. We can see beauty and we can create beauty. It comes in many forms, forms we are all familiar with. Not only that beauty which an artist creates and shares, but also in the mother who nurtures others into wholeness, the father who provides his family with security and peace, the friend whose faithfulness gives hope, the stranger whose smile lights up the day. And these are all acts of giving. And in giving it away, your beauty generates more beauty in this universe. As a reflection of God's beauty, you are not only the partaker of that beauty but the conveyer as well. "The soul will behold in herself the mountain flowers mentioned above, which are the abundance, grandeur, and beauty of God."[7]

Beauty can take us by surprise as it appears in places we never would have dreamed. Image a flower making its way through cement gracing us with beauty in spite of its struggle to survive or the gem-like crystal inside a dull geode.

Years ago I volunteered to spend a summer assisting

our missionaries in Peru. We worked and lived in a little village north of Lima. It was my first experience visiting a developing nation and I can still remember my first hours there. The government had imposed a curfew because of the activity of the Shining Path, a communist militant group. Though we had arrived at three o'clock in the morning, the sisters and I could not leave the airport until five o'clock, two hours later. The progress of our driving along Route 1 matched the slow rising of the sun. With every mile the woven huts and wooden shacks became more visible and the shock of what I saw more powerful. We arrived at the parish house where the Sisters lived, which seemed just a bit more equipped compared to the living conditions I witnessed along the way. That is to say, the Sisters had electricity from seven o'clock until nine o'clock in the morning. and again for two hours in the evening. The few villagers with electricity got it by way of battery power. The villagers had no water except the one well in the center of the village. The water supply was rain water on tap; however, everything had to be boiled three times for drinking or cooking.

One day while I was alone in the house, some village women came to the door. Even with my limited ability to speak and understand Spanish, I was able to detect that they wanted me to follow them. After a five-minute walk with this entourage, we came to a two-room house. We walked through it to the back yard which amounted to a walled-in dirt yard. There, adorning the mud brick walls, were the most beautiful creations, the women's hand-embroidered cloths, mostly threaded patterns on white muslin. It seemed from their gestures that they wanted me to judge their works. But every time I pointed to a piece of embroidery and said: "Que linda!" they gave me that piece. So arrogant and insensitive of me! What they had wanted was for me to select what I liked as a gift to bring back to the United States. I went home with an armful of lovely linens and a tearful memory of the beauty that came from such external poverty. I recognized that feeling of being in touch with God's beauty, the beauty that emanated from these village women.

These women and you have a great thing in common—the spiritual genes of our Father and Mother Creator. Though worlds apart, these sisters of ours reminded us that we are indeed the beauty of God, and the well of our own inner beauty is reflected in the works we do.

A Meditation

BEGIN your time of solitude with the mantra: "I am beautiful." Continue to breathe the words in and out, slowly, until you begin to believe in the words. Ask God to help you with any unbelief. Later, as the day progresses, say these words as often as possible before you speak to any person.

7

YOU ARE GOD'S COMPASSION

Be compassionate as your heavenly Father is compassionate.

—Luke 6:36

*J*eanne was at a school luncheon explaining to a teacher how she came to adopt her two beautiful boys, Andrew and Steven. Her eyes lit up as she told how she and her husband were watching a special on television one evening when a report came on showing the conditions in the orphanages in Romania under the Ceaușescu Regime. That report moved her to tears, and that night, as she lay in bed wide awake, she asked the Lord for direction concerning what was heavy on her heart, the sad lives of those Romanian children. The next morning, she said to her husband, "Honey, I think we should adopt one of those children before another one dies from neglect." Together they prayed, again for direction, and became resolute in their desire to adopt. Jeanne's call to the local television station began the long journey that led to the adoption of first, Andrew, and then Steven. What is it that moves some people to have that kind of compassion, to go so far as to change their entire lives for a stranger in another country prompted by a TV program? What kind of resolve does it take to move a mountain for the sake of another? It takes great compassion.

Compassion is not just a thought or a feeling but an action of love. It means being disturbed down to your very toes in a way that makes your feet move toward that person or creature in need. It means that a surge of energy and a desire to help, flows out to your fingertips.

Jesus was standing in the village street when a funeral bier passed by. He looked over to the procession and saw the mother of the deceased sobbing inconsolably. The woman did not see Jesus for the tears that were blinding her. Perhaps Jesus was thinking of his own mother at that moment, as with a pained heart, Jesus moved toward the woman, desiring to help. From the very depths of Jesus' being came a spirit that gave life to the diseased young man. In bringing the man back to life, He brought a future back to the man's mother as well. The Gospel pages are infused with many such stories revealing Jesus' compassionate actions.

A person who modeled such compassion, who lived in our time, is Dorothy Day. She was the cofounder of the Catholic Worker Movement through which she mirrored the compassionate Christ. She lived in New York City and traveled the United States by bus, eating peanut butter sandwiches. Dedicating her life to the pursuit of social justice, she was in complete solidarity with those who were considered the misfits of society. People were in awe of her commitment, but Dorothy Day did not want her life to be seen as above someone else's. She told people not to make her a saint because she did not want to be dismissed so lightly.

It's true. We sometimes dismiss the challenges in someone's life by simply stating: "Well, that person is a saint and I'm no saint." We might think that person's way of life is so unattainable and so extraordinary that we could never do something similar, and we then distance ourselves from the challenge. But we cannot disregard the poor and marginalized as "someone else's concern."

A compassionate heart is able to embrace even those who are unable to reciprocate. Such love is inclusive. That's why Day brought people to stay at the Catholic Worker Houses. At one point, when Day insisted on extending their hospitality to those addicted to alcohol and to prostitutes, the core residents of the Catholic Worker Houses refused to continue supporting Day's mission. But looking upon Christ on the cross, Day was able to stay resolute in reflecting the compassion of Christ to all those who were marginalized, including addicts and prostitutes.2

Once we start looking for compassion in the acts of those around us we become aware of the variety of ways in which it is shown. It can be a simple word or a sacrificial act. This past year I was invited to a luncheon for Darlene, an award recipient who had done much to assist the sick, the elderly, and the young in our community. After the award was given we were served our meal. While we were eating, a woman came to our table and asked to see Darlene for a moment. I saw them talk, hug, then laugh, but it wasn't until later that I learned who the woman was. Darlene explained that when she was seven years old she received a bicycle for Christmas. A few days after Christmas her father approached her with a request: would she consider giving her bicycle to another little girl who did not get anything for Christmas. Darlene had always looked up to her dad, but she thought her heart would break when she gave away her new bike. She never met the girl who was to get this great gift. It was this early experience that taught her how to be generous and to reach out to a person in need. Now here she was, sixty years old, a lifetime later, and who should find her but the very recipient of that bicycle! How ironic that this happened at an award luncheon recognizing Darlene for her generosity. This was the first time that the bicycle recipient could thank her. She knew it was Darlene who gave her the bike because the woman's father, an immigrant from Italy who was out of work that Christmas fifty years ago, had told her the bike came from another family from Italy. She knew that her father had been a good friend of Darlene's father. She meant to write Darlene during all those years but only knew her maiden name and had no way to connect with her. That day at the luncheon, as the woman listened to Darlene's history, it all came together.

Because we bear the image of Christ, we have the potential for the compassion of Christ. God's spirit is in us, continuing to reach out as God would. When compassion is felt deeply, our action on behalf of another has a lasting effect on us. Meditation on our past or that of another can bring us to the light and memory of compassion. It can open for us footprints of compassion to follow in our own lives.

My sister, Pat, worked in an orphanage throughout her high school years and after. Sometimes she brought one of the children to our house for an afternoon. I was not much older than these children but was deeply affected by the idea that they had no parents. What's more, when I went to the orphanage with my sister and saw the rows and rows of beds and cribs, of toilets, of tables, and of lockers, an image was imprinted on my little person that still disturbs me today. Though I was little, the images have remained emblazoned in my mind. The sorrow I felt for those children who had no mommy or daddy recurs every time since when I have visited an orphanage. It is what moved me to volunteer as a tutor in an orphanage when I was a teen. I believe it was a large part of my joining the Sisters of St. Francis that I might reach out in compassion to those in need.

It was this concern for others, in part, that led me to join the Secular Third Order when I was in high school. Part of our program was to do service for others beyond our family. My choice was to tutor at The House of Providence, an orphanage for children aged seven to sixteen. I was assigned to work with Tommy, a nine-year-old boy who, along with his five-year-old brother, had been abandoned by their addicted mother. They were left in a house during the winter where the temperature fell below freezing since they had no heat. Because of this, Tommy got sick and lost hearing in one ear. A neighbor, who observed the two boys coming and going in and out of the house without any adults, saved Tommy and his brother by alerting the authorities to their plight.

Knowing about Dorothy Day, knowing what Noreen did, having worked with Tommy, and having visited our Sisters' missions in Africa and Peru, I will continue to replay stories of how others are truly Christ's hands and feet for those in need. Images of suffering often haunt us and motivate us to reach out to others. God brings us to this awareness of other's needs and put compassion in our hearts that we might be moved to serve.

Ralph Waldo Emerson once penned: "If I have made life better for at least one other person, then I know I have lived."[1] When we are compassionate, we have made life better for two people: the person in need, and ourselves.

A Meditation

Write the names of five living people who model compassion for you and indicate why. Thank them when you have a chance, and thank God for them.

8

YOU ARE GOD'S MOTHER, BROTHER, SISTER

He said to the one who had told Jesus that his mother and brothers were outside: "Who is my mother? Who are my brothers?" Then, extending his hand toward his disciples, he said, "There are my mother and my brothers. Whoever does the will of my heavenly Father is brother and sister and mother to me."

—Matthew 12:48–50

*J*esus in this quote is using the language of intimacy, a way of exposing God's heart of love. Jesus spent the whole of his ministry inviting others into a relationship—"that all of them may be one, Father, just as you are in me and I am in you. May they also be in us so that the world may believe that you have sent me" (John 17:21).

We reflect a God who is in relationship by nature. The Trinity, three in communion with one another, reveals that we, too, are meant to be caught up in the relationship of this mystery. It is humbling to think that the God who created us, who is All Good, All Knowing, All Powerful, wants a relationship with little old me and you. But that's why Jesus came. Jesus was in relationship with everyone, most especially those who were told by society that they do not deserve to be in relationship.

My earliest recollection of being in relationship came when I was standing on the counter of my grandmother's kitchen at two or three years old. I was crying my head off because my mother was not there. She had left me to stay with my grandmother overnight. It was sheer terror to be "abandoned" by my mother. Such a symbiotic relationship with our mothers soon opens to include our fathers and siblings, then other relatives, friends, and the community. Our confidence grows as we experience the mutuality of love. We are also consoled as we realize that we do not have to carry our burdens alone nor celebrate our joys in solitude. Every stage of spiritual growth brings us to the primacy of relationships.

God, who knows everything about you says: "I want an intimate relationship with you." The idea of a mutual relationship with God is particularly stunning. "What could I possibly offer God?"

As an evening prayer, one of the sisters with whom I live suggested that we each relate something that God thanks *us* for. I was startled at the idea. God thanking me? My thought was: "If I did something good, kind, or loving during my day, well, wasn't that just what I am supposed to do? Besides, there are probably too few of those instances anyway." When it was my turn, I said the first thing that popped into my head: "God thanks me for calling on an elderly woman today." The prayer got me thinking that God thanks us all the time for lots of things. God thanks us for trying our hand at something new or stretching our abilities and talents. God thanks us for daily things we do or take on in order to make life better for someone else. God thanks us for making mistakes and learning from them. God thanks us for being faithful, for trying and for being ourselves. The possibilities are endless.

God needs you to be in relationship with God because it is the only way you will discover who you really are in this grand march of life that leads back to the heart of God. You are a particular image of God with a particular way of showing God's love. If you turn your back on this call to relationship, then hundreds, thousands of people and generations of people will be affected. It sounds a bit far-fetched doesn't it? But the decisions you make today have a direct effect not only on the people of your time but on the days to come. You influence more people than you are aware of, often just by example, leaving a legacy despite yourself.

St. Francis had this effect on many people who watched what he was about and how he had given his life to God. A wealthy, handsome young man, Bernard of Quintavalle, invited St. Francis over to dine with him. Bernard, a long time buddy of Francis, was curious as to why Francis left everything to follow the way of Jesus. During the night when Francis thought Bernard was sleeping, Francis got up, knelt, and prayed aloud to God. Bernard, who was feigning sleep, saw the sincerity of the little man of God and made a resolution to follow him, giving up all he had to live the Gospel.[1]

Francis continues to influence people of all faiths, eight hundred fifty years later. Everything in creation became his sister or his brother. He knew we are all intrinsically related, to one another and even to the creatures. Clare of Assisi, the first woman to follow Jesus in the way that Francis did, wrote to one of her sisters, "You are spouse and mother and sister of my Lord, Jesus Christ, be strengthened in the holy service begun in you out of a burning desire for the Poor Crucified."[2] For Clare, Christ is the mirror we must look at every day and continue to reflect His likeness in ours.

ONE DAY while I was walking the beach, I asked an elderly man who was building a sand castle how the construction was going. He responded, "Well, I'm learning a lot about foundations!" His words gave me pause. What about our foundation, what is at the heart of each person? Foundational to our very being is the fact that we are held at all times by a God who is "brother and sister and mother" (Matthew 12:50) to us. We are scooped up into a primary relationship with God.

PERSONS WHO ARE DYING and have no primary caregiver —that is, a relative, significant other, or friend who is the number one person caring for the dying person— are frequently referred to Francis House. The very first resident who came was Ken, a man who had been living at the Rescue Mission and who was now very sick with lung cancer. He wanted to continue to smoke so the volunteers wheeled him outside and visited with him while he smoked. Ken was a quiet and shrunken man, aged before his time and was with us only three weeks. During that time, Ken shared his story, a story he had not shared with anyone. The reality was just too painful to talk about. Because he trusted the volunteers, he opened up. Ken had grown up with an abusive, alcoholic father. Ken, himself, became addicted and because of that was dishonorably discharged from the army. The shame of it all led him to seek help. With sobriety attained, he met and married a "wonderful" woman who gave birth to a beautiful little girl who was the "apple of my eye," Ken explained. His daughter was killed in a tragic car accident at the tender age of five. The loss was too much for this already fragile man. He started drinking heavily and his life spiraled out of control. His wife left him. The bank claimed his house. So Ken took to the streets where he was living until he was brought to the Rescue Mission. One day, as I entered Ken's room and went close to him I saw big tears running down his face. When I asked what was wrong he said, "It's too much. I can't believe people would love me like this." Ken died a week later.

His funeral was at the Sisters of St. Francis Mother-house Chapel and celebrated by the staff and volunteers of Francis House and some of the Rescue Mission clients. It was standing room only in the large chapel which seats two hundred. This is what Christ meant about being His mother, brother, and sister.

Jesus said that his mother, brother, and sister is anyone who does the will of God. In saying that, he was not diminishing the role of his own mother, Mary. She, in fact, was the first one in Jesus's life to carry out the will of God. What is the will of God for you? The bookshelves in local stores are filled with books telling us what our purpose is, how to find meaning, and where we should go for answers. Yet, Jesus could not have been clearer. The words Jesus spoke were inspired by God, whose will we are seeking. "Love your enemy" (Matthew. 5:44). "What you do for the least . . . " (Mt. 25:41). "Love God with your whole heart, soul, mind, and strength, and your neighbor as yourself" (Mt. 22:37). It is all about being in loving relationships. When we are taking care to love the "least" among us and even the enemy, we are truly then loving God with our whole heart and soul.

A Meditation

As you allow yourself some solitude space, ask the

Holy Spirit to bring to your mind the names and faces of those who have become family to you because of shared Gospel values and or activities. Give thanks for this family. Pray over who you are to Jesus: a brother, sister, mother, father, daughter, son.

9

YOU ARE THE GRATITUDE OF GOD

Go back and recount all that God has done for you.

—Luke 8:38

oes the grateful person receive more blessings because he or she is grateful, or is that person just more aware of blessings that any of us might be? Is it awareness that makes the difference?

A WOMAN STOPPED to talk with me after a liturgical service to tell me she has had nothing but sorrow in her life. She had her childhood stolen from her by the early death of her mother, she worked long, hard hours all her life, and raised three children. She went on to say that her husband died four years ago, her son lost his job, she had to sell her home and move to a senior person's complex, and her body was riddled with arthritis. I couldn't help thinking that there must have been some blessing in her life somewhere, at some time! Perhaps she was blind to her blessings that day because of her pain. I cannot judge but sometimes we cling to those events that brought us sorrow or pain. This pattern of thought can hold us in bondage.

Sometimes we see ourselves as "victim." Our refrain is, "Why does it always happen to me?" Or perhaps it's about "waiting for the other shoe to drop." For those who proclaim "death always happens in threes," I always wonder what set of three they are working on. These are all ways that some people look upon reality, singling out events that have made them suffer. They lock into a negative memory, to be remembered over and over again, reliving it in an overall negative pattern that becomes their lives. I have sat with dying people who have told me they are grateful for their disease, for they did not live fully until this came upon them. There are those who find blessing in the midst of tragedy and sometimes throughout a series of losses. These are the people who count blessings, not troubles. Their perspective on life is one of gratitude, not anger. It is not possible for anger and gratitude to occupy the same moment in your life or the same space in your heart.

There is a wooden cup on my prayer table made by a housemate, Jeanne. She once made a similar cup for us to pass around a feast day table. Each person at the table was to share a blessing in her life for which she was grateful, drink from the "Blessing Cup," then pass it on. It is a beautiful custom, she explained, dating back centuries in the Polish tradition. Every morning, since that feast day, I simply look at the wooden cup on my table, mentally raising it to God in thanks for five things for which I am grateful that day. Every day the "thanks" are different. Some of my blessings are as basic as the sun's rising, the night of rest, my morning coffee, or last night's dinner. Some days when I am not as sleepy, my blessings may have more thought behind them. One day I shared this daily practice with one of my prayer companions. After a bit of thought, she responded, "That is so proactive! I tend to thank God at the end of the day for something if I think of it. But doing it in the morning will open me to thank God ahead of time for what the day will bring!" I never thought of this daily ritual as proactive, but then again, God has always been proactive. Saying the meal blessing prayer, "Bless us, O Lord, and these Thy gifts which we are about to receive from Thy bounty, through Christ, Our Lord. Amen," is as appropriate for when we go for a walk, drive in our car, look out at a vista, or visit a museum as it is before a meal. God is the One who gave everything in the first place. We can never get a jump on God's generosity! God will never be outdone in goodness and kindness. I can give nothing to God that God hasn't given first. What I have found is that this simple ritual gives me energy, opens my mind to blessings throughout the day, and prepares me with positive awareness just as that woman observed. The bent of my heart is changed, which in turn changes my whole outlook for the day. Starting our day with thanks doesn't mean we won't have days that are upside down. But it does mean that an underlying peace and spirit of thanks are more pervasive than those times of disturbance. Those dark moments do not become the "theme song" of our days and years. This is evidenced by the lives of those around us who exude positive regard for their lives and for the world around them.

A beautiful man, Mr. Dickens, lived next door to our family when I was a kid. Living in an apartment complex afforded us only a tiny yard. This generous neighbor used to let us kids come over and play in his yard when he was outside, which, weather permitting, was daily. Once we saw him, we ran over to be with him.

Mr. Dickens would sit and watch us as we gathered up the chestnuts from under his big tree. He laughed at our antics while we made bracelets and necklaces with the chestnuts. Frequently he would take us up the long stone path in his garden showing us the differing beauties of each flower and teach us their names. He pointed out the goodness of the plum trees that in season gave us fruit to eat. Mr. Dickens opened our eyes to see how gifted we were, and all the while gave us the greatest hugs. We never knew he was legally blind. I cherish the fact that I have a photo of my five-year old self taken on Easter day in his yard. Mr. Dickens was an Easter person, full of joy and thanksgiving. Without being direct about it, he taught us to be grateful for the beauty around us, for flowers and trees and soft grass. His gratitude was contagious, and we three little children caught it. Mr. Dickens was a blessing in our lives and I am sure, by the way he showed us affection, we were a blessing in his.

In Jesus's last discourse, he prayed to our Father: "I have made your name known to those you took from the world and gave to me . . .. I am not praying for the world but for those you have given me . . .. Keep those you have given me true to your name . . .. I pray not only for these, but for those also who through their words will believe in me. Father, I want those you have given me to be with me where I am." (John 17:6, 9, 11, 20). Jesus sees the early disciples as gifts. He considers all those who follow in the same Gospel Way as gifts. You and I are a gift. Here is Jesus, about to be tortured and executed, but his heart remains full of gratitude for all the Father has given him. The discourse also reveals gratitude for a mission completed, a mission of teaching us that everything comes from a loving God.

Where there is gratitude, there is a reflection of God. What better exercise is there but to recount daily the people, the occurrences, the surprises, the beauty the day brought to us, letting our hearts overflow with gratitude.

A Meditation

BRING a cup to your meditation corner. Ponder the many blessings that have been spilling over that cup throughout your life. Write down as many as you can think of during this sitting. Then write your own prayer of gratitude to the Giver of all gifts.

10

YOU ARE THE DIVERSITY OF GOD

When he comes, being the Spirit of truth, he will guide you to all truth.

—John 16:13

G od loves diversity. God made diversity! The beauty of this universe is based on diversity. We are exposed to diversity from the beginning of life. Our siblings are different from us, as are the members of our extended family. Our friends, the people in our neighborhood, our co-workers all look and act differently. It couldn't be any clearer that God delights in variation—just go to an aquarium, to a zoo, or a large flowering garden, and you will see and delight in the differences. My surroundings exposed me to this truth at a very young age.

My three sisters, parents, and I lived in a two-bedroom, cold-water flat attached to several other apartments in a residential neighborhood. We saw our neighbors' comings and goings. One of those neighbors was Stella, an exotic dancer. When I was very young, I didn't know what Stella did for a living, and sure wished I could have sparkly dresses like the ones she hung out on our porch to air! Then there was Gracie, a woman we called Spindles because she was so thin. My mother trained me to refrain from eating the candy she had in pretty dishes all over her apartment unless she offered it. I did a lot of praying in her apartment! Bunchie and Bobby were my playmates, living in the two front apartments. I knew that each of these people was different but never gave it much thought. In college I roomed with a Puerto Rican girl and years later taught in an inner-city Puerto Rican community. This was followed by six weeks working with our missionaries in Peru, then chaplaincy in two hospitals, two years as a companion to persons who had AIDS, and for the last thirty years I've worked with many people from diverse backgrounds, all of whom were dying. It often felt like the "envelope was being pushed" because I was being stretched. Could I see the face of God in each of these? Often I missed it because the differences became a threat. When we compare, we can feel threatened. Our ego says: "Is he smarter, is she prettier, is that one holier? Are they right, and does that make me wrong?" The comparison can also lead to the illusory thinking that I am superior, or that I am not as good. These thoughts often lead to the building of a psychological wall where we no longer invest in relationships with those who are different. Then again, everyone is different, so who and how do I choose to build a relationship with?

Franciscan theologian John Duns Scotus wrote that each of us has a "thisness" about us. 1 The Latin word he used was *haecceitas*. It is that unrepeatable, once-in-this-universe part of our being that no one else has. It goes deeper than looks, personality, or intelligence. In fact, it is known only to God. But it is what makes us this person and not someone else. It is that part of us which is eternal. The Jesuit poet Gerard Manly Hopkins was so on fire when he read Scotus' thesis about "Haecceitas", he wrote the poem "Kingfishers." In the poem Hopkins proclaims, as did Scotus, that each thing acts to reflect its own being: a kingfisher makes radiance, a dragonfly makes iridescence, stones make wells echo, bells toll, and a good man does justice.[1]

In other words, each thing does its being. Everything

has a nature peculiar to itself. It is faithful to existence when it is faithful to that nature. Christ is true to His nature in the face of every person, meaning that the image of God is in each person and therefore each person is called to "Godness."

One of the early residents we were privileged to care for at Francis House was an Italian born man, Salvatore, who spoke broken English and beautiful Italian. A cloth merchant in Italy, he'd had a successful career because he charmed his customers with song. He made up and sang a different song for every color and texture of cloth in his shop. His delightful songs expressed a heart that also delighted in the richness of diversity. He was God's minstrel celebrating the many and varied expressions of the created world. Sal used to sing his songs around the dining room table as he held up cloth napkins. I smile and give thanks as I think about this faithful disciple of God.

God's call to you is like God's fingerprint on you. There is nothing in the universe exactly like you. God loves each of us with a love meant only for us. There are no two dandelions alike, no two snowflakes, zebras, leaves, or trees, or anything else. Even identical twins are different. A careful study of their physical properties will reveal this. All nature bears a specific touch and likeness to our Creator. God calls each of us into a relationship and calls us by a name known only to ourselves and God. When you give God time in solitude, putting your ear to God's heart, you will hear that name. God is calling you into being, into being the specific, unique you that you were meant to be. The closer you get to that real you, the closer you are to God. Jesus is the "thisness" of God, that reality which cannot be repeated. We cannot be Jesus, but we can image God in the way that is ours to do. If you are not faithful in learning how to image God as you were called to, then the world is missing that part of God that only you can show and only in the way you can show it.

St. Francis, when asked who was the most perfect of all the friars responded:

A good Friar Minor should imitate the lives and possess the merits of these holy friars: the perfect faith and love of poverty of Brother Bernard; the simplicity and purity of Brother Leo, who was a man of most holy purity; the courtesy of Brother Angelo, who was the first noblemen to enter the Order, and was endowed with all courtesy and kindness; the gracious look and natural good sense of Brother Masseo, together with his noble and devout eloquence; the mind upraised to God, possession in its highest perfection by Brother Giles; the virtuous and constant prayer of Brother Rufino, who prayed without ceasing, and whose mind was ever fixed on God, whether sleeping or working; the patience of Brother Juniper, who attained the state of perfect patience because he kept the truth of his low estate constantly in mind, whose supreme desire was to follow Christ on the way of the Cross; the bodily and spiritual courage of Brother John of Lauds, who in his time had been physically stronger than all men; the charity of Brother Roger, whose whole life and conversation was inspired by fervent charity; the caution of Brother Lucidus, who was unwilling to remain in any place longer than a month, for when he began to like a place, he would at once leave it, saying, 'Our home is not here, but in heaven.'[2]

Each friar had his own unique beauty, which Francis saw and loved. There were no "cookie cutter" applications, no expectations that the followers of Jesus would be anything other than the person they were called to be. It is not important that we be perfect; in fact, that is impossible. What is important is that we realize how intentionally we were created and intentionally loved.

A Meditation

GO OUTSIDE and pick two leaves (or two snowflakes if it's

winter) that look exactly alike. Look carefully at the veins in the leaves or the shapes of the crystal snow. Give God praise for diversity. Include in that praise the wonderful way in which God has made you unique, with your talents, your interests, your personality, your beauty.

11

YOU ARE GOD'S LIBERATOR

The Spirit of the Lord is upon me . . . he has anointed me to proclaim liberty to captives.

—Luke 4:18

"Give me liberty or give me death," was not just Patrick Henry's cry. These words have reverberated through the annals of history from the mouths of all those experiencing oppression. We have heard it in the colonies at the birth of our nation, on the plantations in the South, in the boats carrying immigrants, in the mouths of captives everywhere. The prisoner unjustly charged cries out for long-awaited freedom. The people involved in civil rights movements around the globe all want to echo Martin Luther King's words: "We are free at last."[1]

Over thirty years ago, I attended a confirmation in Hoboken, New Jersey, presided over by a visiting bishop. His exhortation to the confirmation class was to take their courage from the Lord and stand strong in their faith. He exhorted them to believe that Jesus is always with each of them, just as Jesus promised, and will never let them down. He told them that all they needed to do was to lean on Jesus. The bishop then shared one of the most faith-filled stories I have ever heard. While a military chaplain in World War II, he was captured by the Japanese and interrogated. Because he was an officer, he was not killed but was imprisoned in a cell, the dimensions of which were four feet by four feet, allowing him only enough room to sit or squat. The guards let him out twice a day for five minutes each time. The very meager rations he was given to eat were passed through his cell bars. During the months of his confinement, he challenged himself to stay sane by recounting every step and word of Jesus in the New Testament, everything prophesied about Jesus in the Old Testament, and written about Jesus in the Acts of the Apostles and Letters. Over and over again he journeyed mentally with Jesus. The whole time he was in captivity, he was free because he was not mentally in that prison box. He was journeying with the One in whom he trusted and who makes us all free.

YOU HAVE BEEN MADE in the likeness of God who acts in complete freedom, and in that freedom chose to create you. You are free to choose how you live, what your priorities are, what goals you pursue, and how much you let God be the animator of your life. No matter what your circumstances, you are always free. However, we frequently fail to realize this. We are constrained by our negative thinking, drained by hopelessness, and frustrated by strife. Too often we wall ourselves up in prisons of fear or climb into a hole when our ideals are shattered. This is the human struggle of trying to be who we are meant to be. This effort lasts a lifetime. But when we are faithful to the struggle, we find that with each bend in the road we are freer in making choices. Freedom is ours by our birthright as a son or daughter of God. We, therefore, are free to love or not love, free to be our true selves or free to shrivel up. It is in this great gift of freedom that we can make some very good choices that bring life, and also some poor choices that bring small deaths along the way. But God is ever faithful. No matter what our choices, God continues to draw us forward in love, to bring us to a fuller life.

Jesus was the ultimate liberator. He repeated his message over and over, that God is at all times and everywhere with us, and that there is nothing that we could do to lose God's love. Jesus's responses to violence and persecution were to absorb the evil nonviolently, showing that we are never forced to return "an eye for an eye."(Matthew 5:38) Jesus engaged with those who were poor, diseased, and marginalized, even shunned, by His culture and religion. He knew the law, but chose first the law of love. He chose sinners, commoners, and the discredited to be his followers and spoke of a new kind of vision. His stories came from the streets and fields, not from the temple. He declared that his family members were all those who received his words. He raised the spiritually dead and broke the yokes of those oppressed. As God released the captives of Egypt, so Jesus brought liberation to captives of hate, greed, and every kind of evil. He began the story of salvation history. He announced a year of favor, a time of jubilee, when all was to return to its original state. For us, that means a return to our original state of goodness as a son or daughter of God.

In Victor Hugo's *Les Miserables*, there is a touching scene of liberation. The Bishop offered hospitality to

Jean Valjean, an ex-convict. The next morning, the Bishop learned that his guest had stolen the silver from the cabinet. Shortly after, police brought Valjean, with the stolen silver, to the Bishop. The Bishop told the police he gave the silver to Valjean and then turned to Jean, and in a voice the police could hear asked, "Why didn't you take the candlesticks that I also offered you?" When the police left, Jean stood before the Bishop with head bent low in shame. He asked the Bishop why he lied. "Because," responded the Bishop, "with these candlesticks I have bought you your soul." From that moment of liberation, Jean Valjean became a new man and returned the favor to everyone he met for the rest of his life.[2]

Jean's story reminds me of the true story of Mitch. He is an inmate in a high security prison. He had a violent temper when he was young which got him a life sentence when he took the life of another. Mitch became a friend of mine because of an article in a magazine about the work of Francis House. He started writing to me because he had begun doing hospice work in the prison, inmate to inmate. Mitch took on a ministry of presence to men who are dying of AIDS in the prison infirmary. He says it is a privilege to sit with men in their last days. He explains how he prays with the men, reads Scripture to them, and sometimes just sits with them.

There, in that place of no return, a dying inmate finds God in the presence of another. Spiritual freedom is found everywhere, for God holds it out to us in all times and places. The true disciple leads others to that freedom as well.

It is amazing how being bound up because of our wrongdoing or that of another can cause us to be in psychological and physical prisons. While a hospital chaplain, I encountered a woman who had been a challenge to the doctors. She had stomach cancer but every proven course of action the doctors tried had failed to cure or even help her. With each new therapy she seemed to get worse instead of better. She was admitted to the hospital for more tests when she was unable to eat. My first visit with her found a woman who was pleasant but who volunteered nothing and spoke only in response to me. With ensuing visits, she became more open and friendly, and spoke about the long road of treatment and the difficulty she had had along the way. She was discouraged and ready to give up. One day, toward the end of the second week, well into our conversation, I acted on an intuition. I asked her if there was a heavy burden she was carrying from the past, a pain deep inside that was worse than physical. She broke down and talked for the first time in many years about how she "carried in her gut a hate for the man who raped her granddaughter." She just could not forgive this man for what he had done. It was clear that this had been eating away at her. When she had shared all she wanted to about this crime, we prayed together. I asked her to ask Jesus to be the one to forgive because she could not forgive right now. Every day we prayed the same prayer: "Jesus, forgive in me because I cannot forgive."

Once this woman was able to keep some food down and showed signs of getting stronger, she was discharged. A few months later I heard that she was making progress; her cancer was finally responding to therapy. Indeed, her whole being was responding to the therapy of God's light within her.

We are all prisoners of a sort—locked in our own small ideas, trapped by our addictions, tethered to the expectations of others, or oppressed by circumstances of our lives. The freedom which living in God offers is ours to find. And when we do, we can help to show others the way out of their prisons, too.

A Meditation

IS THERE something that is keeping you bound? Holding you back? Are you wrapped up in fear or adversity, or carrying something that you cannot slough off? Imagine Lazarus being called from the tomb by Jesus. Hear Jesus's words: "Unbind him." (John 11:44) Out of what tomb is God calling you? What wrappings need to be removed so that you may live freely? Write this out in your journal. Close with a prayer asking Jesus to unbind you, and raise you to new life with the freedom that Jesus longs for you to have.

12

YOU ARE GOD'S PRESENCE

And know that I am with you always, until the end of the world.

—Matthew 28:20

a humble little man named Brother Lawrence wrote one of the greatest inspirational works. As a cook and shoemaker, he practiced the presence of God, focusing his mind on the fact that God was with him in each moment. He gave direction to others by way of letters, which after his death became the book, *The Practice of the Presence of God*. In his very simple telling, Brother Lawrence demonstrates that he is aware of God within him as well as his being in God whether he is frying an egg, cleaning a floor, or talking to someone at the door. He reminds us of God's presence by quoting the words from Matthew 28:20: "And know that I am with you always, until the end of the world." Brother Lawrence presses on: "It is not necessary for being with God to be always at church; we may make an oratory of our heart, wherein to retire from time to time, to converse with Him in meekness, humility, and love."[1]

It is very hard for some people to genuinely believe that God dwells within them. It is too much to believe that God is with them, in them, and through them when they feel that they are not worthy. It really is not about our worthiness. Who could ever be worthy of God's choosing to be with them and in them? It is all about God wanting so much to be present to us. God even came to earth to make that happen and put God's own Spirit in each person. But the issue is not God's, it is our lack of awareness and acceptance.

Buddhists meditate to be awake to all life. "Be awake!" the Zen Master would say. The admonition is to be aware of all reality and your presence in that reality until you come to the realization that all is one. There is really only one reality, and it is God. For we who are raised in the Judeo-Christian tradition, this is the greatest truth we could ever grasp. God is in everything and without God there is nothing. God calls all things into creation. All that is comes by the hand of God and continues to be animated by God, for God's very self is within all beings. The essence of God has been given to all that has been and all that will be created. God is by nature love, and love is self-diffusive. God is always giving God away!

At Francis House, we are privileged to often witness and hear the residents' last words. Mary came to Francis House with severe lung disease which made it very difficult for her to speak, for the air she took into her lungs was limited. Her children came from three different states to be at their mother's bedside in her last days. She was visibly waning and the staff of Francis House called her children in to say their last goodbyes. Though Mary was weak and looked quite frail, she mustered all the strength she had to say goodbye to her children. She motioned with a withered hand for them to all come close to her. She looked around at the faces of her children, and whispered to them, "Stay close to each other. Never stop loving one another. You are all precious. I love each of you. Love each other like I love you." Mary closed her eyes and never spoke again. A few hours later she died.

In the Gospel of John, these last words of Jesus are repeated over and over: "As the Father is in me, so I am in you. Live on in my love . .. . anyone who loves me will be true to my word, and my Father will love him; we will come to him and make our dwelling place with him. . . Live on in me as I do in you . . . I am the vine. You are the branches. He who lives in me and I in him, will produce abundantly, for apart from me you can do nothing" (John14:11, 22; 15:4, 5). These words are repeated in chapters 16 and 17 as well. If you believe that Jesus existed and was the Christ, then you have to believe in his words. They carry an urgency to know how present he is to us. A person repeats over and over what he or she wants to make sure another person understands. How can we not fall in love with this God who so wants to be present with us and repeats that in a thousand ways?

In my first year of college I enrolled in a Bible studies course. The final exam was to name all the books of the bible in order. That was it! There is not another thing I remember about that course and I still get the order of the prophets mixed up. We students would have been much farther ahead in life had the professor taught that the Judeo-Christian scriptures are all about a loving God who wants to be present among us, and who asks us to be God's image for others.

God is most present in the everyday stuff of our lives. It is through the dark places in our lives as well as through the light that God speaks. In our culture there is a great avoidance of death, aging, suffering, pain, and even talking about any of these. But it is here that we find who we are in God and how God is in us. It is in persevering and working through the places we would rather avoid that we grow spiritually. An elderly friend of mine has told me a few times already, "You know, I like that new young pastor we have. His homilies are always related to our lives. That's what we need to hear, how God is present now in our reality! Not what God did some centuries ago!"

An art teacher told me over and over again, "Don't be afraid of the dark colors. Use them." What she demonstrated on canvas was that every painting had to have dark hues. It was the dark strokes that gave it texture and depth. While I am painting I have to encourage myself by repeating her words because it takes courage to apply black or any dark color to what your mind tells you is a light color in real life. Painting the shadows on or near an object brings out the contrast and enhances the beauty. This refrain of hers has been a reminder to me about life in general. Don't be afraid of the part of yourself you keep in the shadows; don't be afraid of taking risks; don't be afraid to tread where you have never trod. The truth is, we are mostly in the dark regarding God! We do not have the capacity to know the magnitude of God's love. How could we dream to know this God who is after us?

Francis Thompson's "The Hound of Heaven" is an eighty-two-line poem which describes God as the "Hound of Heaven," chasing us "down the nights and down the days." The poet runs and hides from God but God proclaims, "Naught shelters thee, who wilt not shelter Me." God is the only true source of our safety. In the end the poet has God, the Hound of Heaven speak; "Ah, fondest, blindest, weakest, I am He whom thou seekest! Thou drove love from me, who drove Me."[2] Those who are weak and blind run from God, who cannot see that God loves them so dearly and wants to show that love. They will not find the love they seek because they drive themselves from God. The irony is, the closer we come to loving ourselves, the closer we come to loving God and allowing God to love us. It is when we are practicing this loving presence when we most image God. God dwells in us through the Spirit and that is what makes it possible to give presence to others in whom God also dwells. We are all are connected at the foundation of our being where the Spirit is anchored. It stands to reason then, that God's presence is most felt when we are present to one another.

We must be confident that the indwelling One will

continue to work through us if we are even a bit mindful of that Spirit. When you make the sign of the cross, "In the name of the Father, and of the Son, and of the Holy Spirit," you let go of acting in your name and act under the name of the Three in One who all love you. When Paul and John were at the temple area, they had no money to offer the crippled beggar but offered instead what they did have—faith in the name of Jesus. They were present to the man in God's name, not in their own. They had confidence in the Holy Dwelling of the Spirit, which gave them the power to be a Holy Presence.

When Moses walked up to the burning bush in the desert, he was told to take off his sandals because he was standing on holy ground. The spot where Moses stood was holy because God was with him, surrounding him and working through him. When Moses asked what to say when the people ask what this God's name is, God responded: "I AM." This is equivalent to saying I AM in all time, space, matter, and spirit. I AM all life. I AM in YOU! So God summarily sent Moses to let the Chosen People know that God was with them. God did not and

will not abandon the people. God's "I am" is proof that God is alive, is with us, and will lead us out of bondage to freedom.

Praying over this passage many times led me to use

God's revelation in my morning prayer. When I sit in quiet prayer, I often start with the mantra, "I AM," focusing at first on my breath, then on the breath of my being. God is the I AM in and around me, a presence I can only pray I can bring to another.

God is most present to people in their distress. Presence is what has made all the difference for people who are living their last days at Francis House. So many families have said to our staff, "We could not get through this if you weren't so present to us." This was true with Marie, a volunteer who worked many years at Francis House serving our residents, cooking for them, sitting to converse with them, or just being a quiet presence. Marie was then diagnosed with cancer and in spite of many treatments the disease progressed. Not having anyone at home to care for her, she came to Francis House as a resident. Marie's first words were, "I wanted to come because I knew I would not die alone. I have seen so many people here die in peace and I have always felt the love the moment I used to walk in the door to volunteer, so why would I go anywhere else?" What Marie felt was God's presence in the love and care that she and so many others have given to those who come to live at Francis House.

Christ asks each of us, "May I have the honor of your

presence?" Whether we are aware of it or not, God is always with us.

A Meditation

Allow yourself to be present with your own breathing. Become aware of the constant rhythm. Think of someone who is always constant in their presence to you. This is how God is at all times.

13

YOU ARE GOD'S SUFFERING

I solemnly assure you, unless the grain of wheat falls to the earth and dies, it remains just a grain of wheat. But if it dies, it produces much fruit.

—John 12:24

W hen love gives all, there will be suffering. We love as God loves when we are self-giving, self-emptying. Such a love is like a fountain that overflows all day long, day after day, yet continues to spill over in beauty and delight. By its very nature, love causes us to go beyond ourselves, inconvenience ourselves, and sacrifice from our storehouse of goods, energy, and time. Such a love is not always noticed or appreciated.

I was nineteen when my father died. Shortly after his death I was going through some photos and came across one of him holding me when I was a baby. He looked so very different—young, robust, dark-haired, and standing straight. In less than twenty years he had transformed into an old man. Because of long night shifts, working in temperatures of more than one hundred degrees, and lifting heavy metal sheets to be made into air-conditioning units, he aged considerably. His hair was gray, his body thin and bent, and his color pale. I do not know if it was the hard work or the worry about making ends meet that put the wrinkles in his face. Was it the constant shoveling of coal in the coal furnace which heated our apartment that bent his back or the heavy lifting at the factory? What it taught me was that love costs—often it costs a life. Dad was ushered into heaven at the age of sixty.

MY FATHER'S love for his four girls and his wife pushed him to work beyond his limits and persevere in difficult conditions so that we could have a warm home, food on the table, and clothes to wear. Every parent suffers for the love of their children in order to provide them the fullness of life. Sometimes that love causes hearts to suffer; sometimes it causes more pain than we think we can bear. But that suffering is not unlike the suffering of God. From time's inception, God chose to share love in a way that was self-diffusive. Since the dawn of creation, that self-giving love unfolded in a magnificent story of Presence. "The Word became flesh and made his dwelling among us, and we have seen his glory; the glory of an only Son coming from the Father, filled with enduring love." (John 1:14). Jesus, the Christ, came to show us and tell us very concretely through his presence, words, and works that we are greatly loved. Out of love for us, God gave of himself at the birth of the universe and continues that love story through the stories of a people he calls his own, through salvation history up to and since Jesus came bringing us the message that we are all of God, in God, and with God. It was this love of God in Jesus that brought him to the cross. Jesus's glory was that he succeeded in spending every last drop of God's self on us. On the cross, new life poured out on us. A Spirit of love was passed on to us and remains within us. It is this Spirit that enables us to bring new life out of suffering, new birth out of death.

My hospital chaplaincy included the pediatric ICU as one of my units. One day a beautiful thirteen-month-old baby who had been put on a respirator in the emergency room was brought to this unit. It had happened while returning from a shopping trip. Baby Matthew's mom, Nessa, looked at him in his car seat and saw that he was turning blue. His little head was slumped over. She immediately pulled over, took him from the car seat and tried to revive him. Unable to do so, she raced him to the emergency room which was blessedly only three blocks away. The doctors were able to revive his little heart and put him on life support. For three days, Matthew lay motionless in his crib, a cherub tethered to a respirator. Three brain scans showed no brain activity, so Matthew's mom and dad decided to have the respirator turned off. As I stood by Nessa, whose tears fell upon the beautiful baby she held in her lap, I thought of all the women over time who have held their dying children, including the mother of Jesus. Matthew's heart went on for twenty-five minutes before it stopped. It felt like twenty-five hours. Later that year, Nessa started the first Sudden Infant Death Syndrome (SIDS) chapter in our city. This group gave support to many parents whose children died of SIDS. From that sprang other chapters in our region. Nessa, in her work with young women, became aware of the need to help struggling moms as they tried to provide for their children and established a corporation called "Just for Babies." This agency provided the necessary items for child rearing: bottles, diapers, baby clothing and furniture, and a referral service for the specific needs of particular babies or their mothers. Out of a bitter suffering came life for hundreds of others. I have often thought that the mystery of suffering has something to do with God's economy, meaning much fruit comes from those who give to others because of their suffering. History testifies that from the seeds of martyrs shoots have sprung. It is not that God wills the suffering but that God is in it with us, pulling us through and gracing us to use what we have learned from it. Suffering has a hallowing dynamic to it, which makes room in us for more of God's wisdom and grace. It is in losing that we gain, in dying that we are born. Suffering stretches us beyond the space we once occupied in our minds and hearts. With every experience of suffering there is a new birth; for you can no longer return to the exact person you were before the suffering. Hence, we are changed. With God's grace, if we have endured, we are now wiser, more open, more compassionate, and more able to reflect the image of God. Those who choose to see themselves only as a victim may become bitter, angry, and finally despondent. Only those with hope are able to persevere. Victor Frankl, out of his experience in the Nazi concentration camp noted in *Man's Search for Meaning*: "Hope does not take away the pain and acute isolation of suffering, but draws you beyond the moment of your suffering."[1]

Becky was a coworker who joined our Francis House staff for three days each week. She was a vibrant, enthusiastic woman of forty-five, whose laughter was infectious and whose generosity was overwhelming. Her second year into the job, Becky wrestled with ovarian cancer. This was the third time she had to deal with it, only this time the chemotherapy could not control the spread of the cancer cells. The doctor informed her that she would not live until her daughter's wedding date, which was set for eight months later. Becky broke the news to her family members one at a time and then called a family meeting that I facilitated. She asked me to outline for them how the disease will most likely progress. That evening I took them on a painful journey through the probabilities of their mother's changes, and the physical needs that will accompany them. We then discussed their emotional responses to this heartbreaking news and what they may experience as this process advances. At every bend someone—either me or a family member—suggested coping mechanisms to deal with the trials yet to come. "Where is God in all this?" asked one of the daughters. "Right here, in the middle of this tragedy," I explained. I went on to say that God was walking this road to Calvary again with them, enduring the humiliations, suffering the fall and rise of emotions, inching to the final ebb of life. Becky's greatest sorrow, as she expressed it, was not being with her children and grandchildren as they grew older and especially missing the pleasure of being a grandma to her two grandsons.

Once again, I turn to the analogy of birth coming from loss. A baby does not want to leave the security, warmth, food, comfort, protection, and peace of the womb. Yet, a whole world opens to that child once it emerges from the birthing canal. This new world is filled with possibilities once the painful experience of separation is completed. The baby experiences being held by the mother in a new way, and life itself blossoms toward its own potential. It is the same with death. Death to the womb of this present experience, death to this physical body as we know it can be frightening and painful, but fullness of life awaits us—the completion of life that cannot be known on earth. God is a God of all love. It is not commensurate with this belief to put stock in anything less than the belief that love lives on and grows. The God who loves you more than you can imagine will only increase that experience of love, not isolate you from it. Becky, I believe, is with her loved ones in a much deeper, more satisfying way now that she is free of the limitations of this present womb, our earthly life. Her daughters are delightful, giving young women, who learned much about generosity and love from Becky. They are now walking in their mothers' footprints.

God suffers as we suffer, but God lives and loves as we live and love. What seems like a coincidence of opposites: death to life, loss to gain, suffering to joy, are all part of the continuum we call life with its peaks and valleys. There is diminishment then fullness. Out of our suffering is always the possibility of greater life. "Unless the grain of wheat falls to the earth and dies, it remains just a grain of wheat" (John 12:24). You are God's suffering; you are God's new life.

A Meditation

IT MAY NOT BE an easy prayer experience, but meditate on a past experience that caused you much pain. Try to recreate the event: who was with you, what was said to you, how did you feel? Where was God in this part of your story? What did you learn from that suffering? Has good come from it?

14

YOU ARE GOD'S JOY

As the Father has loved me, so I have loved you, live on in my love. You will live in my love if you keep my commandments, even as I have kept my Father's commandments, and live in his love. All this I tell you that my joy may be yours and your joy may be complete.

—John 15:10, 11

hile visiting a school in Kenya administered by the Sisters of Saint Francis, a companion sister and I led the children in a few choruses of that old 1920's song of George Willis Cook: "I've got that joy, joy, joy, joy, down in my heart, down in my heart, down in my heart." The children sang with such enthusiasm. "Why?" I wondered. These were among the poorest children on the face of the globe. It is because they know they are loved—loved by God, loved by those who care for them.

FROM THE BEGINNING of the story of creation, "God created man (and woman) in his image; in the divine image he created him; male and female he created them. . . . God looked at everything he had made, and he found it very good" (Gen. 1:27, 31). So we are told that God took joy and delight in all things created. Humans, however, are made in the very image and likeness of God, so how could we not be God's joy? God delights in each one of us, loves us and finds joy in us.

That joy reminds me of how my dog, Honey, used to greet me. I could be gone five minutes or five hours and still when she heard me approaching she would begin to dance her "Oh, I'm so glad to see you" jiggle which took up every muscle of her body. Every dog owner can attest to this wonderful show of what looks to me like pure joy.

ASK a mother or father what they feel as they look upon

the beautiful face of their sleeping baby. Is it not a response of joy? This is how God looks upon each of us. More than any loving parent could, God watches over each of us and cares about even the detail of our lives.

There may be someone in your life who you know loves you completely, and in spite of all your quirks and faults, tells you how loved you are and how that love brings them joy. You, too, may experience joy in knowing you are unconditionally loved. The knowledge and experience of this exchange of love moves one to feel deep joy.

According to Merriam-Webster, the definition of joy is "an emotion evoked by well-being, success, or good fortune or by the prospect of possessing what one desires; a state of happiness or felicity, a cause of delight."[1] A person possesses joy as a gift from God because that person knows that no matter what happens in life, he or she is God's delight. Joy does not necessarily depend on circumstances. Joy in the Lord, meaning joy in the Lord's love, is like a river coursing beneath our other emotions. Never had I met someone in whom this is as true as in Pat.

Pat was one of the people I met during a week-long retreat. Though I tried not to look too shocked the first time I saw her, it took me some time to register what I saw. Pat was in a wheelchair because she had prostheses on all four limbs due to overwhelming sepsis which had started as a urinary tract infection three years previous. Over the course of two afternoons, Pat shared that she had been hospitalized and went into a coma. She awakened from the coma one day and was told by a physician that she had to choose between having her hands and feet amputated or die. Pat courageously chose the amputations. More shocking, however, was the joy that Pat exuded. In our conversations, she shared that she could not explain or give reason to the joy that she felt. It was a gift from God. Pat used phrases like "trusting in God," "feeling God's presence," "an overwhelming feeling of being loved," as she smiled her way through her story. Obviously appreciative of every small kindness and of simple beauty, Pat pointed out the flowers in the garden view from her window and the loving care of the staff in her home. One clue to Pat's joy may be the fact that she sits in God's presence for a long time every morning, just absorbing God's love. This is when, she explains, that she most feels God's love. Joy is her testimony to that love. Throughout the course of the week I heard others remark that it is incredible that Pat who has suffered so much seems to be such a joyous person.

IN THE DEAD OF WINTER, while Saint Francis was traveling from the city of Perugia to St. Mary of the Angels directly below Assisi, he was suffering from the cold and was prompted by inspiration to have Brother Leo, his companion, write this description about true joy: "Brother Leo, if it were to please God that the Friars Minor should give, in all lands, a great example of holiness and edification, write down, and note carefully, that this would not be perfect joy."[2] As the journey continued, St. Francis gave Brother Leo other examples that would "not be perfect joy," such as miracles performed by the Friars Minor, even raising of the dead. Nor would perfect joy be caused by having the Friars know all languages, sciences, and scripture, and possess the gift of prophecy. Joy is not to be found in the gift of preaching such that all would be converted to faith in Christ. When the discourse had spread over two miles and still Brother Leo had not been told what perfect joy is. he begged St Francis to tell where joy is. St Francis proclaimed:

If, when we shall arrive at St. Mary of the Angels, all drenched with rain and trembling with cold, all covered with mud and exhausted from hunger; if, when we knock at the convent gate, the porter should come angrily and ask us who we are; if, after we have told him, 'We are two of the brethren,' he should answer angrily, 'what you say is not the truth; you are but two imposters going about to deceive the world, and take away the alms of the poor; begone I say'; if then he refuses to open to us, and leaves us outside, exposed to the snow and rain, suffering from cold and hunger till nightfall—then, if we accept such injustice, such cruelty and such contempt with patience, without being ruffled and without murmuring, believing with humility and charity that the porter really knows us, and that it is God who makes him to speak thus against us, write down, O Brother Leo, that this is perfect joy. . . . if we bear all these injuries with patience and joy, thinking of the sufferings of our Blessed Lord, which we would share out of love for him, write, O Brother Leo, that here, finally, is perfect joy.[3]

At the conclusion of this exchange, St. Francis makes clear that all the grace and gifts we have are from God. To accept even the most difficult circumstances of life while hanging on to the fact that God is right there with us, offering us the grace and courage to push on is the way in which we can give God glory, showing that we trust in God's unfailing love. If in times of trouble we can cling to the fact that God loves us more than we can imagine and return to that certainty with joy, we are then God's faithful children. Life will have its stormy days that may be oppressively dark. There is for each of us during our lives the experience of the valley of death, but there is also the mountain of glory. Moments of happiness, joyous occasions that bring pleasure may alternate with painful disappointment and hurt or loss. Joy is deep within and does not come and go depending on the mood of the day. It is not a fair weather friend. Joy is that treasure buried in the heart of the person who knows that no matter what, in laughter and in tears, God is there too, right in the center of our being. The steady hand of God is beneath and around us at all times, sustaining us with love. This belief is the linchpin to joy.

The Christmas and Easter Seasons ring out with many songs of joy for the incarnation of love among us and the proof that love will always have the victory over death. Our faith in these two key events in the life of Jesus assures us that love in our lives is always ready to be born and will always win out over the darkness. For many of the Francis House residents who die at Christmas time, these two seasons are experienced all at the same time, for they are celebrating the birth of Jesus and the Easter of their own lives. Or to say it differently, their Easter resurrection becomes their birth into eternal life.

One resident in particular demonstrated this confluence of seasons. Rosemary secretly planned that since this was to be her last Christmas she would gift everyone in a very special way. She was peaceful with the fact that her death was imminent. Her heart was filled with joy and gratitude toward those who loved her. Over the weeks preceding Christmas, she dictated heartfelt letters to one of her daughters which would carry words of wisdom, affirmation, and love to her children and grandchildren. For Francis House, the staff and administrators to whom she was so very grateful, she had her daughter buy things needed for the kitchen and living rooms. On Christmas Eve we were all called to the living room Christmas tree to open the surprises that Rosemary had planned for weeks. Through her letters and gifts Rosemary lived on way past the date she entered eternal life. Since she embodied joy, it was joy that she left all of us in our memories of Rosemary. It is joy that is her legacy.

A Meditation

START your meditation by singing a song of joy, any one that comes to mind. Be aware of your spirit being lifted. Sing the refrain of that song a few times throughout your day, your week, as a song of praise to God who has carried you through thick and thin, who loves you in this and every moment. Praise God for the gift of joy.

15

YOU ARE THE HUMILITY OF GOD

I assure you, unless you change and become like little children, you will not enter the Kingdom of God. Whoever makes himself lowly, becoming like this child, is of greatest importance in that heavenly reign.

—Matthew 18:3, 4

*A*s Franciscans, we Brothers and Sisters commit to following the Gospel in the way of St. Francis and St. Clare of Assisi. Francis was awed by the fact that our God would take on our humanity to experience all that we may experience: joy, sorrow, love, hate, hunger, satiety, loneliness, camaraderie, strength, weakness, gain, and loss. Jesus would know pain, humiliation, doubt, fear, anger, thirst, betrayal, degradation, and isolation.

Francis was taken up with this mystery of the Incarnation. He was overwhelmed with the fact that God took on flesh, was born in a humble manner, and died a humiliating death. This preoccupation with the wonder of this mystery is often portrayed in Franciscan art through representations of both Bethlehem and Calvary as the crib and the cross. This awe and yearning to understand pointed to a greater reality—the incredible love that God has for us. Why did Jesus come? Our Franciscan tradition teaches that Jesus came to be with us, to tell us about this great love story between God and all of creation and to teach us to continue illuminating the story. We were created in that Divine Circle of love and are meant to bring all others into the Circle to which we all belong by birthright.

St. Clare, the first woman to follow in the way of the Gospel as St. Francis did, urges her followers to think about the fact that we were made in the image of God. She explained to her sisters in her writings that the closest image of God that we can find is Jesus. He is the mirror of God and the model of humility for us.[1]

Both St. Clare and St. Francis encourage us to meditate on the fact that the God of the Universe came to us as a vulnerable baby, born in a barn and laid in the feeding trough of animals. His poverty was a humility that God took on in Jesus so that no one would feel that they are too lowly for God to love. As Jesus grew into his ministry he associated with those who were poor and embraced the outcasts of society. Finally, Jesus's scourging and crucifixion shows his ultimate embrace of humility

Paul, in his letter to the Philippians, explains that Jesus, though he was a manifestation of God, did not cling to an equality with God but rather emptied himself to take on the form of a servant. This is divine self-emptying, the embodiment of humility. Humility does not come from humiliation, as is often thought, like the time I went to a parking lot and got into the wrong car, embarrassing myself and startling the driver. Humility is claiming who we are in the sight of God. It is facing the truth of our personhood and living each day fully embracing the essence of who we are...a bundle of faults and failings, talents, and skills. We cannot climb out of our own skin and spend our lives impersonating another image of ourselves. We cannot conquer our powerlessness by exerting power and control over others. We cannot fill our emptiness by filling our garages, attics, basements, storage compartments, and bank accounts with "things."

The word humility comes from the Latin word *humus*, meaning soil. Humility requires that we "get down and dirty." We are limited creatures who have a multitude of blessings and gifts, who have God within our very being. But we cannot contain all of God or be God. Humility is rejoicing in the "humus," the soil of our being with both its rich soil and its imperfections. We may possess the wisdom of the ages and have knowledge of some of the universe, but never will it be all there is to know. We may learn how to clone but we will never create from nothing.

I WILL COME to you and share my life with you. I will give you as much of my Spirit as you can experience—that is a paraphrase of Jesus' last message to the disciples (John 14:16). The humble person acknowledges limitations but also accepts all life as a gift. The humble person arises in the morning praising God for a cup running over with the glory of a new day and all it may contain. Humility prompts us to glorify God who creates all forms of life, all acts of love, and all moments of grace.

The gift of humility was given to Earl, learning of God's grace as it worked through another on his behalf. Earl had been sick for some time when he became a resident of Francis House. He quickly grew to love the visits of volunteers and would welcome them with the greeting, "Welcome to my home. This is Love House." He once shared with me that a frequently seen volunteer had been so friendly and warm to him that Earl took a risk and revealed a part of himself he found troubling. He explained to the volunteer, "I don't know how to pray. It has been a while since I have been to a church or read a Bible. I just don't know how to get back." The volunteer said, "Well, I'm no expert but I'll share what I do. I simply kneel at my bedside every night and say, "Well, God, this is the kind of day it's been. I've done these things OK and didn't do these others so well. I'm sorry for those times. But I'm grateful for this whole day that You have given me. Thank you."

Earl was humble enough to open his heart and share his concern over his relationship with God. The volunteer was humble enough to share his "seven loaves and two fish" (Matt. 15:36). This visitor didn't say, "Wait, I'll get a chaplain in here to see you." He simply shared what his experience of prayer was, and in so doing, helped another to take a leap in faith.

You are in the image of Christ when you humbly surrender your independence and recognize your dependence on God. We delude ourselves if we think we can be self-sufficient. Our very breath depends on a loving God. The existence of this world, our common home, depends on the existence of God. Any goodness that comes from my words or deeds comes from the Spirit of this generous God. The patience to endure suffering, the faith to overcome doubts, the hope to believe in second chances, the generosity to give to those in need—these all come from the grace of an abundant God who is within us and around us at all times.

One of the most humble, yet influential people I knew was the janitor of our grammar school. Every day Mr. Wendling would be outside greeting the students by name, one at a time. He noticed the little things about each student and would comment, affirm, or respond to a need. When I lost my little prayer book, it was Mr. Wendling who noticed my distress and asked what the matter was. He went about looking for my treasure. When he found it on the playground, he carefully put it in an envelope and came to my class, asking to see me for a moment. With a big smile he handed me my prayer book. My peace was restored. But my distress was not the only brush fire he put out. Day after day Mr. Wendling served the school and everyone in it, right down to the littlest student. He reminds me of another person, Mary, who worked in the hospital while I was a chaplain. Though her job was cleaning the patients' rooms, she made it a point to bring some sunshine along with her into every room. It was clear that Mary had little education, but this humble woman cured more ailing hearts than most of the Pastoral Team.

"Who we are is who we are before God and nothing more," St. Francis admonishes.[2] You may, in humility, acknowledge that you are nothing without God, but in God, you are great.

A Meditation

Go to your yard and pick up a handful of soil. Examine it closely. Notice that it has a variety of small particles. Notice its color and smell. Pick up another handful of soil. Notice the differences in their composition. When you discard the soil, it leaves in your hand its own residue. It may be called dirt, but its richness brings us life. Consider the similarities between this *humus* and your own life.

16

YOU ARE THE OBEDIENCE OF GOD

*Anyone who hears my words and puts them into practice is
like the wise man who built his house on rock.*

—Matthew 7:24

he word obedience comes from the root,
oboedire, which means to listen. To be in
obedience to God is to truly follow in the footsteps of
Jesus, who reminded people over and over that He was
doing the will of God. How did He know that will? Was
there some special manual, a set of directions in his
back pocket, a recording of instructions? No, no, and no
again. What Jesus had was a listening heart. He went off

by Himself frequently to exercise that listening heart. In solitude God directed Him.

You might ask: "Why doesn't God direct **me** in every little thing? Why don't **I** get messages as to what job I should take, who I should marry, where should I live? Why don't **I** get those messages that tell me what to say to my grieving neighbor, my oppressive boss, or even to the stranger asking for a handout?" Perhaps we don't give time to the Lord—quality solitude time—to listen to what is in our heart. That's how God directs us. Perhaps the noise around us is too loud. Obedience is about listening. We cannot follow the will of God unless we know how to listen. Jesus went away to pray for guidance and to be confirmed in God's life in him, in God's mission for him, in the will of the One who sent him. But Jesus was human. He could not know what was around the bend in the road. Jesus listened long and frequently to understand that God did indeed abide in him, that his mission was to draw all back to God, and that the message was always about love.

We will never know what Jesus heard when he went to the mountain top or into the desert to pray and listen to what the will of God was for him. What we do have are Jesus' words of compassion, forgiveness, trust, exhortation and healing. These were the fruit of his prayer and his way of being the obedience of God, acting on the will of God. Jesus worked out of the Spirit He carried around within Him, trusting in the words of His Father that were spoken and Jesus obeyed.

THE PEOPLE with whom I live take time every day to practice the prayer of contemplation daily, figuratively sit at the feet of Jesus like Mary of Bethany did when Jesus visited the home of Mary, Martha and Lazarus. This was Mary's listening position. This is a prayer of doing nothing but being at God's disposal. It is a way of becoming aware of and marinating in the presence of God. Nothing extraordinary happens during that time, such as hearing voices or seeing visions. Often we are asked: "What does happen during that time in solitude?" To answer, I use a quote from an elderly man: "I look at God and God looks at me." While nothing usually happens during that daily time of solitude, just being aware of God's presence and letting the Spirit wash over you makes all the difference. Hearing God stir your heart, attending to an inspiration, or beginning to see that there are no coincidences, recognizing that God is in everything—EVERYTHING—that's what happens in solitude. There is really only ONE life and it is God's. "For in him we live and move and have our being." (Acts 17:28).

Years ago as I was driving toward the place of my annual retreat, a drive that would take six and a half hours, I was concerned about getting lost. (This was before GPS.) So I was equipped with directions from the internet, and two road maps were spread out over the front seat. Unfortunately, I had no one with me and had never been to upper New Jersey before. Shortly after I crossed the Pennsylvania state line into New Jersey, I started looking for an exit where I could get gas without going miles off the interstate. I prayed, "God, lead me to the right exit." The traffic was heavy and I did not want to lose a lot of time. I skipped two exits and got off at the third, then debated between two gas stations, both at the bottom of the exit. After fueling up at the one that would put me in the direction of reentry to the interstate, I sprawled my maps over the hood of my car. A man pulled over and asked if I needed directions. I didn't need to wonder how he knew, with maps visible at every angle! He had a warm, smiling face conveying kindness and a willingness to help. I explained that I was looking to see where the New Jersey Turnpike began. "Where are you going?" he asked. I told him to Sag Harbor. "Oh, you don't want the Pike! You stay right on Route 80. Where are you going, anyway?" I explained that I was headed to a retreat center on Bay Street in Sag Harbor. To my surprise he knew just where the street was. Mind you, Sag Harbor is not in New Jersey; it is on Long Island, and we were a good three hours from the place. "Here's what you do. Well, wait, I will draw you a map," at which point he jumped out of his pickup truck to draw a map, including shortcuts, to the street I needed to be on. "Jim," then gave me his cell phone number in case I got lost, wished me well, and was off. As I proceeded back onto the interstate, I said: "Thank you, God, for the urge to get off when I did, choose the station I did, and pull out the map as I did, twenty miles before I would have made a major mistake." Some would say that was just coincidental, but for those who believe that God is in all things, God was in this, too.

For the person who attempts to listen and gives time to listening, the Spirit directs in weightier matters as well. Jesus urged the disciples to hear his words and put them into practice. You, beloved of God, are that obedient, listening one when you believe that God is still speaking. Becoming the obedience of God requires that we put trust in the fact that God never leaves us, though sometimes we leave God. The more we listen and follow what the prompting of God is, the more it seems that God is speaking. It's a lot like flexing a muscle that gets stronger and stronger with each use. God speaks through your heart's promptings and deepest desires.

Sometimes we experience a call to do something or

come from prayer with what we think is an inspiration. Perhaps God is asking something of you. But time passes and circumstances change. If it is the will of God, and if we continue to listen, God will continue to call us to the task.

My friend Susan wanted to join the Peace Corps and work among the poor in Africa. However, after college there were loans to be paid off and that meant getting a job. She excelled in her medical research, and Susan's professional life moved along, as did her relationship with her soon-to-be husband. The years passed. When their children left home to begin their careers, Susan approached her husband Mike with an idea to go on a safari in Africa, a vacation of a lifetime. They planned the safari but also planned to give one week to work in an orphanage for children who are HIV positive. The desire from those early years had never left. "If it is of God, it will not fail" (Acts 5:39). Their experience changed them forever. Since that trip and time in the orphanage, they have sent needed medical supplies, raised money, and spoke publicly about the plight of the children in Africa. Susan and Mike plan on returning to Africa next year. Susan listened and when the time was right, the Spirit led her.

Two very good listeners are Elaine and Frank, dear friends of mine and long-time volunteers at Francis

House, who shared their morning ritual as we were talking about routines. Daily, they wake to an alarm, then, even before getting out of bed, say, "Show us what we can do for You today, God." At that they giggled because God never wasted time in making it clear how they could help someone that day. They are very good listeners.

God speaks to us all the time. Listening and following what we think we hear is what makes us the obedience of God. We are never really sure if we are hearing God or our own voice. So why not rely on Jesus' promise to send the Holy Spirit Who will teach us all things. We have to trust, and good will come from that trust. Believing in God's faithfulness, we have to step out and try, even if we aren't 100% sure. The only requirement is for us to be faithful. Following what we think the Spirit of God is prompting us to do will lead us to fullness of life. It will also lead us to the cross because God will speak to us of love, but the world does not want to hear of that kind of love, especially a love of our enemies or of anything that takes away our superiority, comfort, or security. God will speak to us about being loved and giving love. We have been given life that we may give life to others. Listen. God speaks in a whisper. God speaks in a storm. God asks us to listen with the ears of our heart.

A Meditation

Put on a soft piece of music and let the rhythm, the sound of the instruments, the melody surround you. What images arise as you listen? What emotions do you feel? What memories does the music elicit?

In the same way, we listen to God in the music of silence. Quiet the music and sit in the silence. If you have a decision to make, put it before God and promise to be patient and ever listening to God's direction regarding that decision.

17

YOU ARE GOD'S FORGIVENESS

If you forgive the faults of others, your heavenly Father will forgive you yours.

—Matthew 6:14

*a*way to restore goodness is through forgiveness. Jesus offered forgiveness repeatedly. Perhaps no moment is as poignant as that moment from the cross. Jesus understood his glory as giving all he had—revealing a love that was so self-diffusive that it emptied itself totally. Jesus forgave the religious leaders whose idea it was to have him killed. Jesus forgave the cruelty of the Roman leaders who carried out the deed.

Jesus forgave the people of Jerusalem who were complicit in the cruelty. Jesus forgave the denying Peter and the disciples who ran for cover. Jesus forgave all, even Judas. Jesus' love is dynamically alive throughout the ages and extends to every generation. Every person, whether seeking forgiveness or not, is forgiven and every heart that embraces forgiveness is made free. Goodness and wholeness are restored. For some this reality is too hard to be believed.

A central theme in the play, *Wit; A Play* is "salvation anxiety." [1] The main character, Dr. Banning, a fifty-year-old feared scholar and teacher of John Donne's sonnets, struggles through her cancer treatment and final dissolution of her life. The doctors treating her are scholars in the field of cancer research using Dr. Banning's bodily experience as "the book from which they teach." In the end, Professor Banning claims the sad irony that the cold, demanding way in which she taught, void of feeling and emotional connectedness to her students, is the way in which she is now being treated. She is an instrument for teaching. It is with this realization that she has flashbacks of her teaching of Donne's Sonnet 9. It is in this sonnet that Donne voices the observation that lesser things in nature are forgiven: "If lecherous goats, if serpents envious cannot be damned, Alas, why should I be? mercy being easy, and glorious to God." [2]

That is what God does precisely. God forgives freely and pours out mercy abundantly. This is difficult to believe. It is overwhelming to realize that we are totally forgiven our wrongs. The speaker in the Sonnet chose to be forgotten rather than try to embrace what seems too incredible. This is the result of Donne's "salvation anxiety."

For those who do believe in the greatness of God's love and mercy, there is healing and restoration. God's mercy is new every day. The believer is brought to goodness and in turn, reflects the mercy of God as the forgiven who forgives. "And forgive us our trespasses as we forgive those who trespass against us," Jesus prays.

This restoration to goodness was actually made visible through the lives of Linda and Peter Biehl. Amy Biehl, their daughter, was a killed in 1993 while working on a Fulbright Scholarship in Cape Town, South Africa. She had been struggling for civil rights in several villages on the archipelago with the National Democratic Institute for International Affairs. Amy worked against apartheid when she fell prey to the rage of young members of the anti-apartheid movement. Amy was killed by four young men who mistakenly thought her one of the "oppressors," a white supremacist. She was a random target of the energy erupting out of a rally of a Pan Africanist Congress.

Amy's parents visited South Africa frequently in the two months after her death. Those visits were inspired by Amy's journals. They revealed her passion for the people who struggled through each day in South Africa. The Biehls took up their daughter's work for justice. Today with approximately $2.5 million in grants, Peter and Linda are building schools, housing, bakeries, and golf courses on the same soil that received their daughter's blood. They have raised money for literacy projects, job training, and the funding of small businesses.[3]

And they have helped to transform the lives of those immediately involved in the fateful event of August 1993. One of the four was a young paramedic who despaired because he failed to convince the other men that Amy was a "comrade." The guilt he experienced drove him to alcohol. In spite of his self-imposed blame, the Biehls befriended him. They told him to forgive himself because he did all he could. They gave him a job teaching CPR to residents of villages that were miles from a hospital. Over 4,000 residents have been trained to date.[4]

In 1997, the four young men convicted of Amy's murder asked for amnesty from South Africa's Truth and Reconciliation Commission. All four were allowed to do this because they confessed that their crime was politically motivated. They were given amnesty. The

Beihls found it in their hearts to forgive and let go of their hurt and anger and fully supported the amnesty. At the hearing, Linda Biehl hugged the mother of the young man who stabbed her daughter, Amy. The Biehls have since become good friends of the young men, and as one of these men said: "We call them mother and father now. I don't know how they found it in their hearts to forgive us for what we did, but I can tell you it has greatly enriched my life. I will never forget what we did that night, but I will also never forget the kindness they have shown me when they had every reason to hate me."[5]

The forgiveness of the Biehls echoes Jesus' words: "Father, forgive them." This way of forgiveness continues the mission of restoring goodness to this world. When Jesus wanted to show us the extent of o God's forgiveness or the forgiveness that we are expected to show to others, he told the story of the Prodigal Son.

This is one of the rather well-known parables from the Christian Scriptures. It is the story of a son who demands his inheritance only to squander it in a foreign country. Then, in desperation, he returns to his father begging forgiveness. To his shock, his father runs with joy to greet him on the road, calls for the servant to cloak the young man and places a ring on his finger. His exuberance spills into the declaration of a party. Jesus is well aware that a Jewish father would not run to meet a son who disowned the family or throw a party for one who owes so much. But the story illustrates the lengths to which our forgiving God goes to reach our divided hearts.

It is difficult for any of us to be at peace when we are at odds with another. We carry around with us the burden of a grudge, or a hurt that has not been forgiven. It weighs like a heavy stone precisely because it is *our* hearts that are hardening when we cannot forgive another. We have witnessed eleventh hour forgiveness many times at Francis House as a person strives for peace by letting go of the past, the hurts, or the years of bitterness. It seems to be part of the unfinished business that so often must be tended to before one dies.

Genevieve was lingering beyond expectations because there was someone she needed to see before her final breath. It is like that father looking down the road every day, anxiously waiting for the prodigal. It is usually a child or a sibling for whom a dying person often waits to see, but in Genevieve's case, it was her mother. Genevieve was married to a very controlling husband who years before had a ferocious argument with Genevieve's mother. Genevieve thought it her duty to side with her husband and so a long lasting wall went up between Genevieve and her mother. Genevieve shared her last and only wish with the Francis House staff, to see her mother one more time and ask her forgiveness. One day Genevieve's mother unexpectedly visited Francis House asking to see her daughter. Genevieve's husband, who was usually at her bedside, was not there because of an appointment he had. Genevieve was asked if she would like to see her mother. When she said yes, her mother was escorted to her daughter's side. Mother and daughter hugged and cried together. Genevieve died in peace that night.

A Meditation

Get a sheet of paper. On it write the name of someone you need to forgive but don't think you can. Lay the paper down, as if you were laying it at the feet of Jesus. Ask Jesus to forgive that person, working God's grace through you. When you are ready, take the paper back and write "Thank you" across the name on it.

18

YOU ARE GOD'S HOPE

"For I know well the plans I have in mind for you," says the Lord "plans for your welfare, not for woe! Plans to give you a future full of hope."

—Jeremiah 29:11

The people of the Hebrew Scriptures had hope in the God who was leading them. God had led them out of the terrible trials and woes of slavery in Egypt. God was leading them with a pillar of cloud by day and a fire by night. They had the certainty that God was with them and would not abandon them. Based on the many ways God had shown care and love for them, the Hebrews hoped for a better day, for freedom and new life, for joy and peace.

Think for a moment about the leaders that God worked through. Abraham and Sarah were an elderly couple who had moments when they abused others, but they became the parents of many generations of believers. Their great grandson, Joseph, was a conceited dreamer but he saved his people from famine. Moses was a stutterer, a murderer, but listened to God's instructions and led the Israelites out of bondage. David, another murderer and an adulterer, became a great king who called his people to faithfulness, praise and obedience to God. The smelly, disdained shepherds were the first to hear of the Good News of Jesus's birth. Peter was a headstrong fisherman who denied Jesus but became the "rock" of the early church. Francis of Assisi, my father in religion, was a playboy and "wanna-be" knight who became a knight of the cross and who, still today, draws others to follow in the footprints of Jesus.

How can we doubt that God can work through each of us? Our hope lies not in our abilities, but in the fact that God chooses our lowliness, our weakness, to reveal goodness and strength. My favorite line from all of scripture is: "Glory to Him whose power now at work in us can do immeasurably more than we ask or imagine" (Eph. 3:20).

Symeon, (949–1022 A.D.), known as the New Theologian, comforts us with these words,

"Everything that is hurt, everything that seemed to us dark, harsh, shameful, maimed, ugly, irreparably damaged, is in Him transformed and recognized as whole, as lovely, as radiant in His light.[1] God places hope in each one of us and never gives up. There is nothing we could ever do that would make God love us less.

There are times in our lives when the darkness seems to overcome us and hope may be more elusive than ever. Each of us will have circumstances that cause suffering, crises that seem crushing, losses too difficult to bear. We pass through these times and try to put our lives back together. New visions of what can be start to rise. Hope is God's grace pulling us through to another day and lifting our heads to the future.

Sylvia was a person of hope who had a way of passing on her positive energy, igniting hope in others. She was my housemate and through her I found that my own sense of hope grew, and saw the same happen to others she touched. We were blessed by the way she believed that good will win out, that new realities are possible, and that life comes out of suffering.

A poem that captures and honors Sylvia's life was

written by Grace Noll Crowell. It is a poem about a violin.

The Stradivarius

Long centuries ago it stood—a wonderful thing;
A tree pregnant with the voices of the rains and seas,
Swept with the passion of the wind's wild melodies,
Bowed with the grief of storms, and stilled to slumbering.
Drenched with white moon showers, and called upon to sing

...

Then came an hour—the axe, the shrieking fall,
The travail—and a violin drew breath
To sigh and sob and sing of life and death;
A glorious interpreter of all
Dreams, delight, despair, that holds for me
Heartbreak, beauty, and a strange wild ecstasy.[2]

SYLVIA ENTERED the Sisters of St. Francis at the same time I did; then thirty-seven years later we lived together again. She played the violin and taught English literature. On her fiftieth anniversary as a vowed religious sister, a Mass of celebration was held. The violin was played and her friends put on a skit playing the parts of various poets: Frost, Whitman, Emerson, and Shakespeare. The music and play were a nod to her various talents and ministry, underneath it all, I observed a steadfast hope as her source of energy. Sylvia believed in a struggling student; survived through the treatments of her first and second bouts with metastatic cancer; and stood in the face of adversity as an elected leader of the congregation. She even named a new convent Our Lady of Hope. She infused hope in the sisters of our religious congregation and gave presentation after presentation promoting a new union with other congregations of the Franciscan Order. She was an activist for social justice, protesting in Washington against the School of the Americas, and locally involved as a member of the Syracuse Peace Council. Throughout all difficulties, she never lost hope.

Throughout her last years of life, Sylvia ministered as a visiting chaplain, a program she started as an outreach of a home care agency. She selflessly served patients even while suffering through her own treatments. Louise, a woman with advanced ALS and her husband, John, who cared for her, were often the subject of Sylvia's remarks on courage. Louise did all she could to live a full life even though her only remaining ability to communicate was blinking. Sylvia saw in her what she unknowingly displayed to others, a hope and courage to keep going. Sylvia often gave courage to our adopted cocker spaniel that trembled at the slightest noise or appearance of someone new. Actually, Sylvia was afraid of dogs, but once we brought this cute little one home, Sylvia's fear melted away. She named the dog Honey, would invite Honey into her room, and looked for her when she came home from work every day. One day I came home and found her bathing the dog! Sylvia had moved from fear, to courage, to hope.

The day Sylvia collapsed on the floor, after having vomited blood, she was admitted to the hospital. The news came that nothing more could be done; the cancer was too advanced. A Sister friend of hers and I fretted over telling Sylvia that she could not return home. As we entered her hospital room a big smile came over her face as she said, "I am so glad to see you! I have something to tell you. I have decided to go to Francis House as soon as they will let me. I am ready." Sylvia knew Francis House, our home for those who are terminally ill. So many of the patients she had visited at the hospital came to live their last weeks at Francis House. Sylvia taught the volunteers of Francis House in a training class entitled, "The Spiritual Needs of the Dying Person." Now it was her turn to be cared for. Once Sylvia came to Francis House, her health declined very quickly. She never complained. Her interest was always in the person who came to see her. Sylvia's last three days were sprinkled sparingly with moments of consciousness. Her friends sat vigil and held her hand through the final moments of life. As she took her last breath, Sylvia's life of hope was rewarded. She opened her eyes, sat up in bed, smiled and held her arms out straight to be welcomed by someone on the other side of life.

"But hope is not hope if its object is seen; ....and hoping for what we cannot see means awaiting it with patient endurance. (Romans 8:24) Hope is the ground beneath us, that which holds us upright as we put one foot in front of the other while our eyes focus on a distant place. Hope brings the sprig of green out of a withered stump. Hope pushes the athlete to get up again. Hope defeats the naysayers when presented with a vision of what can be. Hope names the next possibility.

When my mother was newly diagnosed with advanced cancer, she smiled at me and said, "Where there is still hope, there's life!" Being young, shaken and inexperienced, I doubted her words. Now, thirty years later I can say, "Yes, mom, there is always hope." God comes through with an abundance of grace for those who hope.

During my training as a sister, I worked as a nurse's

aide taking care of our sick sisters in the infirmary. I learned on the job. At the end of my second year it was time to choose a path: either teaching or nursing. I was asked by the nursing supervisor why I didn't choose to be a nurse. My response was, "I feel so powerless when people die. I can't do anything."

And God laughed. Because twenty-one years later I was given permission to pursue Project Home which became Francis House. It was to be a home where people could die in dignity surrounded by the unconditional love of God. It was hope that sustained me and our committee of advisors when there was no model to follow, no money for the project, and no place to house Project Home. Hope kept the dream alive. Today Francis House is thirty years old.

A funny thing just happened. While writing this chapter I received a note of thanks from Theresa Wolf, author of *Hope in Our Final Season* and the founder of another home for those who are terminally ill.[3] It was hope that moved in her heart. It is hope that is in the hearts of all those who have started homes across the United States for those who are terminally ill and cannot be cared for at home. It is hope that moves us to work toward a day when there will be such a loving home in every city across the country.

Hope is the gift given to us and the blessing we

confer on others. Joan Chittister, Benedictine Sister, once said that "hope is the cutting edge of vision. It tells us that, indeed, another world is clearly possible but just over the horizon. The call of hope is to move toward it 'til we can all grasp it together."[4] We can build that new day as we walk in the light of hope.

A Meditation

TREAT yourself to a meditative walk outside. As you look down at your feet recall a journey you have taken into a relationship, a project, or an adventure during which hope kept you going. Be aware that God is right beside you and always has been. Give thanks.

19

YOU ARE GOD'S CARRIER OF THE PROMISE

I send down upon you the promise of my Father.

—Luke 24:49

*P*arents love their children because the children came forth from them and remain a part of them. When they look at their children they see an image of themselves. When God looks at us, God sees God's image in us. The ever good God has placed the same goodness in us. That is the kernel of truth that Jesus and every mystic since have tried to tell us. Our goodness is a reality precisely because it is God's goodness.

Sometimes you are not even aware of God's goodness within you and even less aware of the effect it has on others. In the late 1970s I taught in a grammar school in Hoboken, New Jersey's inner city. A seventh grader named Prior struggled to learn. He was a quiet boy who never caused any problem. Unfortunately, Prior failed math and had to go to summer school. Twenty years later, I learned he had died when his mother wrote to say, "At the end of the year you gave him [Prior] a small box. Inside the box was a small note folded up. It read: 'Dear Prior, you're a good boy and that's more important than Math in God's eyes. Have a good summer.' Well, Prior passed away in September 2000. When I was going through his things in his room I found this note from you. He kept it all those years!" Of course I had no idea that a bit of affirmation would have a lifetime of importance. We never know how God will use us as messengers, carriers of His love.

God sees God's self reflected in us and calls us forth to show others this truth in them. We are chosen to be messengers of God's love. Each of us does this by pure example and by the way in which we regard others. How else will others know that they, too, are loved and chosen from all time to be created in that love? "As you sent me into the world, so I sent them into the world. And I consecrate myself for them, so that they also may be consecrated in truth. I pray not only for them, but also for those who will believe in me through their word"

(John 17:18–20).

Now being chosen may feel like a very tall order. "I'm not perfect," you may say, "so how can God choose me?" Well, it's not up to you to be perfect; all you have to be is human. God will make up what is lacking. Because it is not about you; it is all about God. God loves through you. But for God to choose you, you have to choose God. That is your part; you have to say yes to God.

Once you say yes, God is with you all the way, never abandoning you. You are called as part of the Chosen People throughout human history. In Genesis 10, God tells Noah that a covenant is being made with God's people. The sign of that covenant is the rainbow in the sky. "See it and recall the everlasting covenant that I have established between God and all living beings—all creatures that are on earth" (Gen. 9:12). The covenant between God and the people is passed on. "The Lord, our God, made a covenant with us at Horeb; not with our fathers did he make this covenant, but with us, all who are here today" (Deut. 5:2–3).

Mary, the mother of Jesus, understood what it meant to be chosen. The angel never said she was picked because she had royal blood, or accomplished great things with her life, or was perfect in any way. No, the messenger said God favored her, God had chosen her. It was not a reward for something she did. The invitation hung in the air like fireworks the second before they light up the sky. Mary asked for an explanation since she had not lain with a man, and did not understand how she could bear a child. The angel said she would be overshadowed by the Holy Spirit. What's more, the angel said, Elizabeth, in her old age would have a baby, too. Then, a reminder: "for nothing is impossible with God." (Luke 1:37) Mary, although shocked by these announcements, trusted this God of the covenant and so responded: "Let it be done to me according to your word." (Luke 1:38) And Mary immediately gave witness to the goodness of God when she visited Elizabeth. Elizabeth, who was granted the gift of pregnancy even though she was beyond child-bearing years, declared herself and Mary blessed for what had been given them. They experienced themselves as chosen. They were to each carry a special child who would bring the Good News of salvation to the people. God had promised from the beginning of time to be with the people, a promise in which both Mary and Elizabeth had a significant role. But each of them, if they could speak to us today, would say that we, too, have a unique opportunity with our lives to carry on that promise of the loving presence of

God. Our election as a carrier of the promise will take place in a way that weaves through the events and occurrences of our particular time.

This election of Mary and Elizabeth was bigger than either of them. They understood this call was not for them alone but for the people of God. It was within the history of their people; God always worked within their reality. Mary, for her part, proclaimed God's greatness and God's mercy in choosing a relationship with her, a "lowly servant" (Luke 1:48). She declared how blessed she was, for God was doing great things for her. Holy is God's name, she said; she did not declare her own name as holy. She professed God's mercy would reach all ages, confuse the proud, depose the mighty, lift the lowly, provide for the hungry, and send the rich away empty. Elizabeth declared that the child in her womb leaped for joy on hearing Mary's voice when she greeted Mary. This was a foreshadowing of the role that Elizabeth's baby would play as the prophet who announced the coming of the Messiah.

Mary and Elizabeth knew themselves to be carriers of the promise. Anyone who is open to God, anyone who believes God's spirit is in them, is chosen to be a carrier of the promise.

That's not to say we will not struggle once we say yes to God. Mary had great joy but she also had great suffering. "One runs the risk of weeping a little, if one lets himself be tamed."[1]

The struggle comes not only from outside ourselves but from inside as well, for we will always be tempted to pull back, to judge, to get even, to be prideful, to be negative, to fall into our personal ego-satisfying agendas. When you make yourself usable to God, there will be challenges to your comfort, your routine, and your expectations. As Potok says, "When I was old enough to understand, he [Chaim's father] told me that of all people a tsaddik [carrier of the tradition] especially, must know pain. A tsaddik must know how to suffer for his people, he said. He must take their pain from them and carry it on his own shoulders. He must carry it always."[2]

A Meditation

THINK for a moment of a family tradition that you have carried on and shared with others. In that case, you were the "carrier of the promise" in the sense that all that tradition has meant through your history and perhaps the history of those before you, you have brought a precious experience to your world. Now, as you sit in God's presence in silence, ask God to reveal to you the ways in which you have brought others to a loving relationship with others, with creation, with themselves, which is another way of saying, with God. In so doing, you are fulfilling your election as a carrier of the promise.

20

YOU ARE GOD'S WITNESS

You must bear witness as well, for you have been with me from the beginning.

—John 15:27

When I was a very young teacher with only two years of classroom experience, I was surprised by a subpoena I received at the end of the school year. I was to appear in court regarding the custody case of one of the girls in my second grade classroom. Terrified is a mild description for how I felt, being so inexperienced and so totally surprised by the circumstances around this legal action. The father of this little girl was fighting for custody of his daughter. Throughout the previous year he would ask me, as a concerned parent, how his daughter, Mary, was doing. I thought he was working with Mary's mother to help their child who was having great difficulty getting to school on time, finishing her homework, or remembering various papers that had to be brought in over the course of the school year. Mary was a quiet child but also seemed generally out of focus. Little did I know that Mary's father was jotting down every detail of our conversations—the date, time, what was said—throughout the year to be used against the child's mother in the courtroom.

"Truth, what is truth?" (John 18:38). I could not be a witness to the appropriateness of either parent. All I could do was question who had the child's best interest at heart. For I, too, had felt betrayed and deceived. Since that time, the understanding of "witness" has brought that courtroom scene to mind.

JESUS, in the Acts of the Apostles, is quoted: "You will receive power when the Holy Spirit comes down on you; then you are to be my witnesses in Jerusalem, throughout Judea and Samaria, yes, even to the ends of the earth" (Acts 1:8). Since that time when the first witnesses were send forth, there have been a great multitude of witnesses. The phrase "cloud of witnesses" refers to these holy ones who have been faithful in giving witness to the Good News of Jesus Christ. Through the centuries the people of God have sung or prayed the Litany of the Saints. We praise those who have been faithful believers and who laid down their lives in one way or another for the Gospel. We all could list people who we would praise in our own litany of holy ones who have given great examples of what it means to be a witness.

We are surrounded by those who have "loved tenderly, acted justly, and walked humbly with God" (Micah 6:8). These witnesses, who gave testimony to Christ while they were alive, surround us in order to help us, to intercede for us, to inspire us. They are not just near in memory, they are actively present in spirit, leading us on the right path. Their testimonies to the God of Life continue to echo through the ages. In John's Gospel, Jesus proclaims: "My testimony is greater than John's: the works my Father has given me to carry out, these same works of mine testify that the Father has sent me. Besides, the Father who sent me bears witness to Himself" (John 5:36). Jesus was sent to reveal the goodness and love of the Father, the source of all that is good, the infinite, and unconditional. Ours is to accept Jesus.

Ours is to believe Jesus's testimony as the truth and to follow in his Way which leads to life.

Jesus testified in his words that this love is all inclusive. It is without end. It is not earned. It is freely given. This gift of love is continuously overflowing, bringing us good. This love is a sharing in the very life of Jesus and in the life of our living God. It is a grace available at every moment.

WITNESSING to God's intent of love, equality, and opportunity for humanity comes with a cost. In his autobiography, Martin Luther King, Jr. explained that when the marches and nonviolent protests began, so did the threatening mail, phone calls, and acts of violence against him and his family. Once in the dead of the night, at two a.m., the phone rang. Martin scrambled to answer it. The ominous voice at the other end said with intent, "You F—-ing N-----! If you don't stop we'll take care of your wife and kid." It wasn't the first phone call like that. But this one shook him to the bone. He did not want to wake his wife so he went down to the kitchen and made coffee. As he sat at the kitchen table drinking the coffee, he suddenly threw himself into prayer: "Oh Lord, why? What am I to do? Please help me. Show me the way." In that moment it came to him that he was baptized in the same baptism with which Jesus had been baptized. He shared the same grace, and the same help would be offered to him that was given to Jesus. From that moment, whenever Martin was afraid or doubted his call, he proclaimed: "Baptismo sum, baptismo sum." (I am baptized, I am baptized). It was a source of both strength and consolation and a witness to the power of God working in the lives of those who believe, Martin is now among the many in the cloud of witnesses.[1]

Someday I think Ro will be too, though she may never be well known and no one may write about her life. Ro is a great witness to the staff of Francis House. Recently, I asked Ro to go sit with one of our residents who had terminal restlessness, an agitated state indicating that death is near. Ro went in, sat down next to this man and started reading from the Bible on his night stand. Later when I walked by, she was holding hands with him and his son, all heads bowed, as Ro led them in prayer. As Ro was leaving at the end of her volunteer shift, I thanked her for having the courage to pray with our resident and his son. She responded: "It is a delight and privilege for me to share the love of God." She continued, "A while back there was great turmoil in my family because of some hurtful decisions our daughter had made. I wanted to remain close to her but could not condone what she had done. Then I prayed to God for peace, and kept praying." At that moment Ro broke into a wide smile and her face lit up like a surprised child. "God touched me with His love. I felt like just the tip of His finger touched me and I was totally immersed in love. I had no capacity to harbor any grudges or judgments, only goodness and love. I can never forget that feeling and remain absorbed in the fact that God bathes me in goodness and love." Ro's face was as radiant as I imagine Moses's face was when he came out of the tent that God had descended upon. Ro is a powerful witness with a surety of God's presence that animates her actions and words. I knew I was talking to someone who received the call to be a witness and who carried it out as a privilege.

There is a holy exchange between God and the person giving witness to God. The power of the Holy Spirit, God's Spirit, rises within the believer and the fire of faith is reignited. "For to the one who has much, more will be given" (Matt 13:12). In exchange, a breath of the witness's spirit is blown into a world suffocating on doubt. God's light comes through this witness and dispels the surrounding darkness.

Every day we encounter witnesses whose love brings life to others, whose faith engenders perseverance in others, whose truth provides clarity to the confused, whose self-giving fosters generosity, whose right-eousness calls others to consciousness. Are these witnesses not the disciples of the Spirit?

A Franciscan Friar, Father André Cirino, started a retreat center in the Bronx for those who are poor. The center, called The Little Portion, was to be housed in a former convent, but before they could move in, a tremendous number of repairs were necessary. Volunteers came forward to repair walls and pipes. Forty people came to paint and others collected furniture. Finally, just before it was opened, the windows were being cleaned. In one of those windows, the friar got caught. The window gave way and came down on him. Fortunately, he was not seriously hurt. The decision was made to buy new windows to avoid the possibility of this happening to a retreatant. But where would they get the thousands of dollars needed to replace over fifty-three windows? The friars and volunteers put out a letter to friends, and within three months, new windows were installed.

The day after all the painting was done, a rainstorm revealed leaks in the roof. Groceries arrived that morning, donated to feed those who came for retreats. As the core group unpacked the groceries, cries went up to heaven: "God, we don't need groceries, we need a new roof!" But at the bottom of the last bag unpacked was a card wishing the core group well with this new endeavor along with a $1,000 check, the exact amount needed for the roof! For every new appliance needed, the money came. To heat the building and feed the people who came on retreat, the friar's province gave the center a check for $19,000 for the year. This was amazing. Father André s dream for his community was coming true. But one day, as Andrè was driving on the New York State Thruway, he heard a voice within him say: "Give the check back." He was startled, but turned the car around and went back to the retreat center. The Little Portion core group gathered and he told them what he had heard. To his amazement, instead of telling him he was crazy, they agreed that they must take the risk and trust in God to provide, and not lean on the assistance of the Franciscan Provincial funds. This act of faith carried them through a ministry that lasted eight years. Father André talks about this story when he preaches to people about faith, but in the very telling he stands as a witness to the goodness and abundant generosity of God.[2]

In 1992 five sisters from the Adorers of the Precious Blood congregation were working to help the people in Liberia. The Liberian military had turned on the peasants at the order of a corrupt government, and in their fervor, the religious were persecuted as well. These five sisters chose to stay and help the poor people instead of fleeing. They committed to witness to the love and faith-fulness they had been teaching. Two of the sisters were shot while driving a catechist back to his home, and a third was killed when the military broke into the convent. Their witness to God cost them their lives but their martyrdom won countless Christians who will never forget their lives of courage and their message of love.[3] They spoke with their lives, a final statement about the Spirit in them who will not abandon God's own. "Therefore, since we are surrounded by so great a cloud of witnesses, let us also lay aside every weight and sin which clings so closely, and let us run with endurance the race marked out for us." (Heb. 12:1). We may not be required to give up our lives to witness our commitment to Gospel values but we are asked to witness by word and action.

A Meditation

TODAY IS a new day given by God's gracious love. Think about what is ahead of you today, who you might be with, what tasks are on your agenda. How will you give witness to God's greatness today? Will it be through prayer offered for someone, a gesture of kindness, a cause you take up?

21

POSTSCRIPT

I live in Syracuse, New York, about ten miles from Chittenango, a village where Lyman Frank Baum lived. Frank, as he liked to be called, is best known for his page and stage work of 1900, *The Wonderful Wizard of Oz*. Most of us are familiar with this American classic from which came delightful songs and a story line that bears repeating for the purpose of this book's theme.

The Scarecrow, who Dorothy first meets, is invited to join her on the journey to the Emerald City where the Oz can get her back to Kansas and perhaps give him what he wishes for—a brain. "If I only had a brain," he sings. Yet, it is the Scarecrow who constantly brings common sense to the Lion and Tin Man as they journey along the Yellow Brick Road. It is the Scarecrow that devises a plan to get into the Wicked Witch's Castle. It's the Scarecrow who recognizes that Toto wants to lead the way. And again, it's the Scarecrow who remarks, "It will get darker before it gets lighter!" as they walk through the woods. This character does not recognize that he already has what he wishes for. It is the same with the others.

Dorothy and the Scarecrow meet with the Tin Man who is invited to join the duo because certainly the Wizard will give him the heart he wishes for! Ironically, the Tin Man is the one who proves to be the most sensitive in the group, rusting himself to paralysis with tears. He puts out the fire that the Wicked Witch throws on the Scarecrow, cries when Dorothy can't make it through the poppy fields and is emotional over the gift of friendship they enjoy.

The Lion, a "scaredy-cat" for sure, who joins the group because he needs "c-c-c-c-courage" is the one who takes on the daring feat of leading the brigade into the Wicked Witch's castle where Dorothy is locked in a room under the witch's evil eye.

Finally, there is Dorothy, who only wants to go back home. She seemingly loses that opportunity when the wizard flies off in the balloon he was to transport her in.

At that moment, Glinda, the Good Witch, appears and the dialogue captures what I have been saying in as many ways as I can:

Glinda: "Well, Dorothy, you were wise and good enough to help your friends to come here and find what was inside them all the time. That's true for you, also."

Dorothy: "Home? Inside of me? I don't understand."

Glinda: "Home is a place we all must find, child. It's not just a place where you eat and sleep. Home is knowing. Knowing your mind, knowing your heart, knowing your courage. If we know ourselves, we're always home, anywhere."[1]

We are at home in God for God is at all times everywhere. We carry images of God with us wherever we go. Sometimes we are better at revealing those images than others, but they are there nonetheless. If any chapter in this little book causes you to believe more in your own goodness and beauty, that goodness and beauty that is of God and remains in God, then I will be most grateful.

In his *Confessions,* St. Augustine of Hippo well expressed what it means to be converted to the idea that we are made in the image of God and it is God who dwells within us: "Late have I loved you, O Beauty ever ancient, ever new, late have I loved! You were within me, but I was outside and it was there that I searched for you. In my unloveliness I plunged into the lovely things which you created. You were with me, but I was not with you."[2]

ABOUT THE AUTHOR

Kathleen Osbelt is a Sister of St. Francis of the Neumann Communities living with two other sisters of St. Francis in Syracuse, NY. Born in Syracuse, NY, Sister has taught in New York and New Jersey. In 1983, she received her MA in Pastoral Ministry and Counseling from Boston College followed by certification as a chaplain. She has served as chaplain in hospitals and as a volunteer in the "Buddy" program for the AIDS Community. It was her experience with those who are sick that led her to found Francis House, a home where those who are terminally ill can live their last days in a loving environment. Kathleen has just retired from serving as the Francis House Director of Mission Outreach and as a founding Board Member of OHN, Omega Home Network, a network of leaders from homes for those who are dying. Sister is also a retreat leader and has given presentations in the United States and in Italy. Kathleen is living with Stage 4 liver and lung cancer which has heightened her conviction of everything she has written in this book about God's great love for each one of us... and for those with eyes open, we see glimpses of that every day

NOTES

You Are God's Dream

[1] G. K. Chesterton, *Orthodoxy* (West Valley City, Utah: Walking Lion Press, 2008), 108.

[2] Mohandas K. Gandhi, *An Autobiography: The Story of My Experiments with Truth*, First Beacon Paperback Edition, (Boston, MA: Beacon Press, 1972), 503.

[3] Joseph M. Marshall. *The Lakota Way: Stories and Lessons for Living* (New York: Penguin Compass, 2002), 27.

You are the Light of God

[1] Raymond A. Moody Jr. *Life After Life* (Covington, GA: Mockingbird Books, 1975). This is a five-year study of the

common experiences of those who have died, experienced life after that death, and have come back to life and related their experiences.

[2] Henri J. M. Nouwen, *Clowning in Rome* (Westminster, MD: Christian Classics, 1992), 101.

You are God's Healing

[1]Julian of Norwich, *Showings: The Classics of Western Spirituality*, translated by Edmund College and James Walsh (Mahwah, NJ: Paulist Press, 1978), 130.

You are God's Beauty

St. Bonaventure, *A Forty-Day Journey into God with Saint Bonaventure*, translated by Josef Raischl and Andre Cirino (Phoenix, AZ: Tau Publishing, 2012).

[2] ANGELA OF FOLIGNO, *COMPLETE WORKS*, TRANSLATED BY Paul LaChance, The Classics of Western Spirituality (Mahwah, NJ: Paulist Press, 1993), 63.

[3] O.A.Bushnell and Sister Mary Lawrence Hanley, *A Song of Pilgrimage and Exile* (Chicago, Illinois: Franciscan Herald Press,1980), 308.

[4] Eric Doyle, OFM, *St. Francis and the Song of Brother-*

hood and Sisterhood (St. Bonaventure, New York: Institute, St. Bonaventure University,1997), 42.

[5] Jan Swafford, *Beethoven, Anguish and Triumph* (New York, New York: Houghton Mifflin Harcourt), 856.

[6] Henri J. M. Nouwen, *Clowning in Rome* (Westminster, MD: Christian Classics, 1992), 101.

[7] John of the Cross, "The Spiritual Canticle," in John of the Cross, The *Collected Works of St. John of the* Cross (Washington, DC: Institute of Carmelite Studies, 1979), 567.

You are God's Compassion

[1] Ralph Waldo Emerson, quoted in *Homiletic* 7, no. 3 (July-September, 1995): 40.

You Are God's Mother, Brother, Sister

[1] St. Francis of Assisi, *St. Francis of Assisi: Omnibus of Sources*, edited by Marion A. Habig, (Chicago: Franciscan Herald Press, 1973).

You are the Diversity of God

[1] Gerard Manley Hopkins, *Hopkins: Poems* (New York: Alfred A. Knopf, 1995), 18.

[2] St. Francis of Assisi, "Mirror of Perfection," in *St. Francis of Assisi: His Life and Writings*, translated by Leo Sherlay-Price (New York: Harper, 1959, p.1218-1219).

You are God's Liberator

Martin Luther King Jr., *I Have a Dream: Writings and Speeches That Changed the World*, edited by James M. Washington, (New York: Harper Collins, 1992), 106.

[2] Victor Hugo, *Les Miserables*, edited and abridged by Laurence Porter, translated by C. E. Wilbur (New York: Barnes and Noble, 2003), 62–63.

You are God's Presence

Brother Lawrence, *The Practice of the Presence of God: The Wisdom and Teachings of Brother Lawrence* (Wildside Press, 2010), 28.

[2] Francis Thompson, *The Hound of Heaven and Other Poems*, (Westwood, N J: Fleming H. Revell, 1965), 11, 18.

You are God's Suffering

Viktor Frankl, *Man's Search for Meaning* (New York: Simon and Schuster, 1959), 132.

You Are God's Joy

"joy." *Merriam-Webster.com*. Merriam-Webster, 2011. Web. 8 May 2011.

[2] Anonymous. *The Little Flowers of St. Francis*, (Garden City, NY: Image Books, 1958), 58.

[3] *Francis and Clare the Complete Works* (Ramsey, New Jersey: Paulist Press, 1982), 165.

You are the Humility of God

Joan Mueller, *Clare's Letters to Agnes Texts and Sources* (St, Bonaventure, N Y: The Franciscan Institute, St. Bonaventure University, 2001), 95.

[2] Armstrong, Regis. *Francis and Clare the Complete Works* (Ramsey, New Jersey: Paulist Press, 1982), 33.

You are God's Forgiveness

Edson, M. (2013). *Wit: A play*. Winnipeg: Media Production Services Unit, Manitoba Education.

[2] J. Donne, Sonnet "Holy Sonnet 9".

[3] Jim Jeter, "Capetown, South Africa," Washington Post Foreign Service Correspondent, Sunday, Feb. 18, 2001

[4] Ibid.

[5] Ibid.

You are God's Hope

Symeon, The New Theologian, "We Awaken in Christ's Body," Poetry Chaikhana, Sacred Poetry from Around the World, www.poetry-chaikhana.com

[2] Crowell, Grace Noll, *Poems of Inspiration and Courage, the Best Verse of Grace Noll Crowell* (New York: Harper and Row, 1965), 157.

[3] Wolfe, Teresa, *Hope in Our Final Season* (Maticus Productions, 2016).

[4] Chittister, Joan, *The Monastic Way* 25, no.1 (2016), Benetvision, January 23.

You are God's Carrier of the Promise

St. Exupery, Antoine de, *The Little Prince* (New York: Harcourt Brace Jovanovich, 1971), 86.

[2] Chaim Potok, *The Chosen* (New York: Simon and Schuster, 1967), 278.

You are God's Witness

Clayborne Carson, *The Autobiography of Martin Luther King, Jr.* (New York: Warner, 1998), x.

[2] As told me by Andre Cirino, OFM, and recounted in Toni Maconi, OSF, *Called To Serve, Birth of A Secular Franciscan Fraternity* (Tau Publishing, Phoenix, AZ) 2016..

[3] Adorers of the Blood of Christ, Liberia Martyrs, http://adorers.org/asc-liberia-martyrs/ .

Postscript

The Wizard of Oz Film, 1939 Turner Entertainment Co. and Warner Home Video, Time Warner Co. The Wonderful Wizard of Oz, 1990, Burbank, CA. Based on L. Frank Baum, Wizard of Oz, Harper Collins Publishers, NY, 1999.

[2] Augustine; Edward D. Pusey, translator, *The Confessions of St. Augustine* (Cosimo Classics, 2006), 188.

Made in the USA
Las Vegas, NV
08 March 2022